W9-AHW-916

An Entrepreneur's
Faith-Based Journey

Angie Cella

RosettaBooks®

NEW YORK, 2021

First edition published 2021 by RosettaBooks

Cover design by Lon Kirschner
Interior design by Christian Fuenfhausen

ISBN-13 (print): 978-1-9481-2281-8
ISBN-13 (ebook): 978-1-9481-2282-5
Library of Congress Cataloging-in-Publication Data: Names: Cella, Angie, author.
Title: Blinger : an entrepreneur's faith-based journey / Angie Cella.
Description: New York : RosettaBooks, 2021.
Identifiers: LCCN 2021021445 (print) | LCCN 2021021446 (ebook)
ISBN 9781948122818 (print) | ISBN 9781948122825 (ebook)
Subjects: LCSH: Businesswomen--United States--Biography.
Entrepreneurship--United States. | Business--Religious aspects--Christianity.
Classification: LCC HC102.5.A35 C35 2021 (print) | LCC HC102.5.A35 (ebook)
DDC 338.092 [B]--dc23

www.RosettaBooks.com
Printed in Canada

RosettaBooks®

Dedicated to Cambria, Christian, Evan, and Grace.

You four are my biggest dream come true. May you each grow up to lead beautiful Christ-centered lives and always shine brightly.

Oh, and I love you more! (I win!)

Introduction

"I came to think of God as more of a gracious friend who was accompanying me on this journey, a friend who wanted to carry my burdens and speak into my life and shape me into who I really was and who I would become."

~**Chip Gaines**, coauthor of *The Magnolia Story* and scrappy *Fixer Upper* guy that everyone loves

It's weird to see people waiting in line to get your product, something you've worked hard to bring into existence and sacrificed so much to get right. It's amazing to think that at this same time last year, no one had even heard of Blinger, the product I invented. Now we've sold over two million of them worldwide. I'm not sure I ever thought it could turn out this great.

But here we are. It's February 2020, and I'm in New York City for Toy Fair. I've been nominated for inventor and wonder woman of the year by Women in Toys. I'm at the awards gala, seated at a large table in the back corner of the room with my children, my mom, my dad and his wife, my assistant and her husband, my attorney, and my publisher. Also, just a few tables over, is the staff of Wicked Cool Toys (WCT), who believed in me and licensed Blinger. So many important people who supported and sustained me along my journey.

I'm up against top players in the industry, including key product innovators with Mattel, Disney, DreamWorks, Hasbro, and Viacom, and I'm prepared to lose. Before our meals are served, Michael Rinzler, president and cofounder of WCT, comes over to our table, and with his signature humor and kindness, says to me, "You don't have your hopes up, right?"

"No," I tell him. "My hopes are appropriately low. I don't even have a speech ready."

The event begins, and my category is first. *Good*, I think.

Though I had already prepared my children that I was most assuredly not going to win, I now had plenty of time before we left to talk to them about the honor of just being in the same group as all these other amazing women inventors.

From the podium, the presenter says, "And the winner is..."

And then I can't even believe what I hear. Did they say my name? I had just taken a big bite of my salad. Now I'm frozen. Nothing was registering.

Then, like in the movies after a bomb goes off and the person standing too close to it can't hear for a while, all the sound starts coming back.

"You won, Mom! Go! You won!"

"I won?"

I have a long walk ahead of me to the stage, and I can't help but think as I move through the room that I also had to take a long walk just to get here now. An amazing journey that started with a dream, and one I can't wait to share with you.

Part of the reason I decided to write this book is I wanted to help others who have a dream, like I did, to have a road map they could follow (or not follow in some cases), to make their dream come true. I don't have all the answers. I'm not some brilliant businessperson or someone who just got lucky either. I've had success because I exert myself, I'm driven, and I've been persistent about what I believe in. But mostly, I had a secret advantage that I can't wait to share with you.

If you want to succeed, you need to be prepared to work hard. I think if you ask anyone who has ever achieved anything big, they'll tell you it took a lot of work. A lot of *ugly* work even. But no one gets to the top of anything without the willingness to do what it takes. You have to be okay with getting your hands dirty, to have people look at you like you've got three heads, to take chances, to have a messy house because you were up all night working on a proposal or a business plan. You also have to be able to steel yourself against the pain of rejection and failure. You can only succeed if you keep going, and you have to believe you can keep going. Belief and persistence are everything.

I believe that God gave me the inspiration to make Blinger in a dream. He gave me this amazing opportunity, and he gave me the tools and resilience I needed to achieve the dream on every step of my journey. I did the work, but Blinger wouldn't be a reality without him.

As with most journeys, a lot of it doesn't make sense while you're on it, and sometimes the true objective isn't what you thought. I thought for years God had wanted me to make Blinger so that I could give money to those in need (and I'm sure that was part of it). But when Blinger became this successful product, it made me want to share my story with others. I wanted to tell everyone what God had done. I think he placed a clear, unshakable vision in my heart, and then purposefully made the road getting there complicated, so that in the end, I'd realize my utter dependence on him. I believe he gave me the dream so I could write this book and share his message with others.

Blinger is the story of my four-year journey to make my product, sharing all the fun and excitement of bringing an invention to life, but also all the work involved—the letdowns, the failures, the tears. I promise this whole thing did not happen how they'd portray it in the movies. In this book, I'll share how all this came together for me, and also some business tips I picked up along the way. I'll also share how my faith kept me moving forward on my journey, never once thinking of quitting no matter how hard things got.

I hope my story will impact you for good and will help you discover God's plan for you. If I succeed in doing that, it will be my greatest dream come true.

Chapter 1

"Nothing happens unless first a dream."

~ ***Carl Sandburg***, American author and two-time
Pulitzer Prize winner

My Blinger adventure all started with a dream. An actual dream I had when I was asleep.

DAY ONE

It was November 2, 2014. In my dream, I was in a sorority house. I was already in my forties at the time, so I'm not sure where the sorority house came from. Plus, I was not a sorority girl back in the day. I went to college on an athletic scholarship for soccer. Still, the images seemed so real.

In my dream, I needed a flat iron. That part made sense. My hair has always had way too much frizz, so I've definitely spent a lot of time straightening it.

I ran into a girl with long, dark, wavy hair (ironically) in the hallway of the sorority house and asked her, "Do you have a flat iron I can borrow?"

She nodded and took me into this large, dark room with lots of wood and three or four beds. There were clothes, shoes, papers, and books scattered everywhere—the way a room might look with several college girls living in it. She led me to a table with a mirror on it and more stuff spread everywhere—brushes, makeup, cotton balls—and handed me the flat iron. Then she was gone.

As I started to straighten a section of my hair, something unusual happened: every time I squeezed the flat iron together, sparkly gems were applied to my hair. I took another strand and ran the iron over it, and again, it left crystals in my hair.

This is awesome! I thought. My hair was getting straightened with an extra bonus of brilliant crystals being added to it. I mean, who wouldn't love that? I remember thinking, *Where did she get this?* and *I need a flat iron like this!*

When I woke up the next morning, I remembered the dream, which was amazing, because how often do we remember our dreams? Occasionally I remember, but not as vividly as this, and rarely right when I wake up. It might come to me later in the morning, or in the middle of the day when I see something or someone that might have been in it, and then it all comes rushing back.

But this one was with me as soon as I woke up. I thought to myself, *How awesome would it be if I made a device that could do that?*

The more I thought about it as I lay there, the more I loved the idea. More than that, I was excited, because I was sure this product didn't exist yet. Not only did I have two daughters, but I was also a vice president with Arbonne, a mostly female network marketing company. I totally would have known if such a thing existed. We Arbonne ladies share our beauty tips and secrets.

I wasn't really looking to invent some new product at this point, though that's not something I'd shy away from either. I just felt that my life was going well at that time. We didn't want for much. Yes, I was a single mom of four kids, but I was making it on my own thanks to my Arbonne business. In fact, the year before, a few weeks after my youngest, Grace, was born, I had bought a beautiful home in Pennsylvania. My Arbonne income helped a lot, but the house had also been in foreclosure, so I was able to get it for a bargain. I was even able to renovate it thanks to a loan from my mom and turn it into my dream home.

Still, the more I thought about it, the more it became clear to me: "I need to make this product!" I jumped out of bed.

It was a Sunday morning and we should have been getting up to go to church, but it didn't look like we were going to make it that day. We had a birthday party to attend that afternoon, and just getting four kids (ages ten, nine, seven, and one—yes, I was a single mother, Christian mother no less, of an infant with a different father than the other three, a man I never married, but that's another story) and myself ready and out the door on time was no easy accomplishment even on our best day—and we still had a gift to buy and wrap.

I felt guilty about missing church. I hate missing it, especially for my kids' sake, even though they love it when we don't go. All but my youngest, Grace. She still loves church and, like me, also feels bad when we miss it. I wish I could be that woman who attends service every Sunday, with all her kids and a husband, everyone looking amazing and all put together, but that's not me. Not right now anyway. I do feel God and I are tight though, and that he's okay with me missing church sometimes. He does want us to come together, and we're powerful when we do, especially in prayer, but he loves us no matter what. You really can't mess it up with him in my opinion. That's what I believe.

Plus, on this particular Sunday, the morning of my dream, I was pretty sure God knew I wouldn't be attending, because I believed the dream came from him.

Let me back it up a bit...

In 2006, I read an amazing book called *The Dream Giver* by Bruce Wilkinson. I started it in an airport in Canada. I wasn't flying home, unfortunately, but to Florida to launch yet another woman into my Arbonne business, which would make it an entire week since I'd seen my children. I was already missing them horribly and was starting to question my decision in working my Arbonne business this hard. I saw a mom traveling with her two kids and just thought of Cambria and Christian (the others weren't born yet). My heart ached and I thought, *I should be home with them, not pursuing this national vice president title.* I was already a regional VP with Arbonne. Wasn't that enough?

The first part of *The Dream Giver* is a parable about a Nobody, called Ordinary, who lived in the land of the Familiar. In this land, when the Dream Giver gives you your Big Dream, he leaves a feather on your windowsill. When you get your feather, you have a choice to pursue your dream or not. Those who do are met with many obstacles, including Border Bullies and Giants, who try to stop people like Ordinary from pursuing their dream. Most of the time, these bullies turn out to be friends and family members who just don't want to see Ordinary get hurt by making what they consider to be a huge mistake. Ordinary has to decide whom he wants to please most—himself, the others, or the Dream Giver. On his journey he learns to put his trust in the Dream Giver.

The next part of the book is about Bruce Wilkinson giving up a position at his church and moving his family to South Africa to launch an organization that eventually mobilized volunteers to plant more than five hundred thousand backyard vegetable gardens for orphans and the hungry. To truly become an evangelist helping people there was his purpose from God.

His story touched my heart and by the end of the book, I was bawling as quietly as possible on a packed plane. Thankfully, I had a window seat. I prayed, though I was not really a believer yet, and asked God to give me a sign. I needed a feather. I needed to know I was making the right decisions for my family as an ambitious working mom.

When I landed in Florida, my friend Nicole picked me up with her little baby girl, Julia, in the back seat. We then picked up her son, Nate, from school, who got into the minivan, not saying a word to anyone. He walked right past his little sister and sat in the third row. He seemed annoyed. We then stopped by the grocery store. Nicole asked me to wait in the car with the kids while she ran in.

A few minutes after she left, Nate spoke for the first time. "Do you want to see my feather?"

I hadn't mentioned the book to anyone yet. I thought I misunderstood him, so I turned around and asked, "What did you say?"

"Do you want to see my feather?" he repeated and held up a paper feather he had cut out in kindergarten that morning.

"Yes!" I said, with my voice cracking and on the verge of another meltdown. "I would love to see your feather!"

That moment resonated with me, as you can imagine. That experience, and other important things that apparently had to happen first, all gave my dream a deeper meaning and made pursuing this product a spiritual one for me from the get-go.

Back to that morning. Cambria, my oldest, was fast asleep in her room. I raced in. "Wake up cutie! I want to put some rhinestones in your hair!" I practically shouted with overwhelming enthusiasm—which tends to be my natural state anyway.

Still not fully awake, she gave me a sleepy, "Huh?"

As a mother of four kids who loves doing crafty things with them, I had plenty of rhinestones in the house. I mean, I *love* creating things. We've made elaborate five-story fairy houses. I've sewn a gazillion Halloween costumes. Once I made a racetrack for my boys in our basement by cutting out the carpet and painting the cement black and adding the little yellow dashes up the middle. For New Year's Eve, I've gotten paint supplies and white canvases and we've had painting parties all the way through to the new year.

"Stay awake! I'll be right back."

I knew I had rhinestones somewhere in the basement, so I raced down to find them. When I got back, Cam had drifted back to sleep, so I woke her up again. I was too focused to let her sleep.

"Come on!" I said and rushed her back into my room. She sleepily sat down in front of her great-granny Grace's chest of drawers and mirror.

As she sat there, patiently, eyes barely open, I started placing the stones in her hair. They had an adhesive on the underside of each stone, so I peeled them off the clear sheet one at a time and tried to stick them onto her hair. I was excited. They looked great! She started to come

Cambria dragged out of bed to get her hair blinged, November 2, 2014.

alive, but she wasn't getting quite yet what all the commotion was about. She was just being a good girl, doing what her mama wanted.

I was happy they were sticking to her hair, but I wanted to make sure they were going to stay in place. "See if you can shake them out," I asked her, and she immediately started shaking her head wildly back and forth.

They didn't budge. I was encouraged. "So far, so good," I said. "Now go play. Go jump on the trampoline! Or do some cartwheels! Don't hold back! Let's see how long they stay in."

She left the bathroom, probably still not sure what was going on. The boys were up by now, so I told them if they all went outside and played, we would skip church. They all immediately raced out the back door. So easy being a mom.

I figured all the rhinestones would fall out, but they didn't. Cambria must have jumped on the trampoline for at least an hour, but the stones stayed in.

Later that morning, when we were getting ready for the party, I realized we had to take the stones out, because in all my excitement, I hadn't thought to brush her hair first. (Tip: Always brush your hair before blinging.) This would not have been a big deal if we didn't have anywhere to be. We probably would have gone the whole day without anyone brushing their hair.

As we headed back upstairs, I was starting to feel a little sense of dread. What if it was difficult to take them out? I mean, after all that shaking and running around, she didn't lose one stone. What if they don't come out—or it hurts? Or what if the adhesive damages her hair? My mind was racing and my mom guilt was kicking in big-time.

She sat back down in front of the mirror, and I started to take them out slowly and as gently as possible.

"Ouch," Cam said after I removed the first one.

"Sorry," I said, wincing now, knowing I needed to continue. My heart was aching as I reached for the second stone. (Please note this was not the safe hair glue we use with Blinger today.)

Before I could get to it, Cambria said, "Hold on, Mom," and she picked up a brush. She ran it through her hair, and just like that, the stones were out. Cambria is so smart.

My enthusiasm was in high gear. The game was on. Now all we needed was a little device that could quickly apply gems to the hair. So simple.

I mean, how hard could it be...?

We were in a hurry to leave for the party, so I didn't have time right then to sit down and figure out this awesome new device I was going to develop. Mom duties came first, so I was just going to have to wait till we got back home. I'm very patient, so this was no problem for me. Ha!

The party happened to be in one of those indoor trampoline places. They had a bunch of games there too, that you could play to win

Toy gun.

tickets. You know what I mean—those tickets you cash in later for little toys and stuff. Anyway, there was this small plastic toy gun behind the counter, and it stopped me.

That's it! We could shoot them in!

I asked the kid behind the counter if I could see the toy gun, and I took a picture of it—of the front and then of the back so I could see where it was made. I couldn't wait to get home so I could Google the company from China that manufactured it and start forging my relationship with them. I was so cute back then.

As soon as I could, after dinner, baths, books, and bedtime, I ran down to our basement again. I wanted to test this shoot-'em-in approach, and I had the perfect "gun" in mind. My mother had owned a garden business that she'd recently sold, so I happened to have a tagging gun, like they use in stores to attach the price tags. I dug it out of a box in our storage room.

8

I realized then I needed a way to feed the stones into the tagging gun. I searched through my kitchen catch-all drawer for something that might do the trick and found a Wite-Out correction tape dispenser. That could do it. I stuck some rhinestones to the tape. I took the tagging gun apart, fed the Wite-Out ribbon through the gun, screwed the

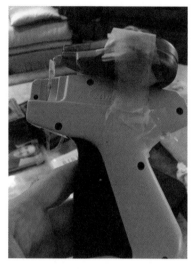

gun back together, and then taped the Wite-Out dispenser to the top of it. Voilà!

I squeezed the trigger and managed to place a single stone onto the surface of our couch. That's when I knew it was totally possible to make Blinger! (Though I didn't know it would be called that just yet.)

But it was November. The start of the holiday season. Two of my children's birthdays are in November, then there was

Tagging gun Wite-Out contraption— the first Blinger!

Thanksgiving, quickly followed by Christmas. As a single mom, it can get overwhelming this time of year (heck, as a married mom it can be overwhelming), and, as parents, all our other responsibilities often take precedence over our personal and business goals. I did some of the preliminary legwork to find an engineer during our busy season, but weeks went by without much really happening.

Then I had another dream.

Chapter 2

"Never give up on what you really want to do. The person with big dreams is more powerful than the one with all the facts."

~Albert Einstein

So I told you that *The Dream Giver* was one of the reasons I saw the dream I had as a possible message from God. But I was actively seeking more spiritual guidance in my life as well at this time.

Earlier that year, at the end of the summer, Cambria and I had decided to watch the movie *Soul Surfer*. We'd seen it before, but we loved it, so we decided to watch it again. If you don't know what the film is about, on Halloween day in 2003, Bethany Hamilton went surfing with some friends and got attacked by a tiger shark. The attack severed her left arm, and by the time she got to the hospital, she'd lost more than 60 percent of her blood. It was a miracle she survived. While she lay there in shock and on the verge of death, one of the paramedics whispered in her ear, "God will never leave you, nor forsake you" (Hebrews 13:5).

Though she was young at the time, Bethany already had a very mature faith. This verse being shared at that moment, whispered in her ear like that, would have held deep significance to her. A reminder that she was not alone, something she would have believed and trusted. Words that would have blanketed her in peace. Thus, placing her in a state that probably kept her alive.

Before the attack, Bethany had wanted to grow and get more serious in her walk. Every night, for about two weeks, she had been praying for

God to use her for his purposes. For God to show his will in her life. Then the attack happened.

To most of us, that would not be the answer we'd hope for from a prayer, but her surviving the attack allowed him to "use her," as Bethany puts it, "in big ways."

Because of her love for surfing, only a month after the attack, Bethany was back on her board in the water. In January 2004, she placed fifth in the open women's division of the National Scholastic Surfing Association (NSSA) regional competition. A year later, she won her first national title by placing first in the explorer women's division of the 2005 NSSA national championships. She went pro in 2007 and still competes today. A one-armed surfing champion.

Bethany started getting letters from all over the world—from children and adults who only had one arm, or one leg, or another disability of some kind. She became an inspiration to so many, and because of this hardship, she was given a stage to share her faith. *That was how God intended to use her.* He knew he could trust her to convey his message to the world. He needed to take her arm to make it happen, but he knew he could count on her to rise above it.

We had seen Bethany speak at this church in our town the year before, but it wasn't until Cambria and I watched the documentary included on the DVD that I learned about the prayer she had been making before the shark attack. It had such an impact on me. I'm not trying to compare my story to anybody else's, but after watching that documentary, I remember thinking, *I want to be used by God too. I would love to be his instrument and fulfill his purpose for my life.*

I already had a purpose. I was a mom, after all. I had everything I wanted right there, but I did want to make sure that I was fulfilling my destiny. If there was a bigger purpose for my life aside from raising my four beautiful children and helping other women build businesses with Arbonne (because Arbonne is fundamentally about helping others), I wanted to know what it was.

I could tell Bethany was much farther along on her walk with Christ than I was, and I longed to have her kind of faith. She was so strong and so soft at the same time. She had a peace about her that I wanted in my own life. I learned in Arbonne that if you want something someone else has, then you just need to do what that someone else does. Duplicate. So I started praying that prayer every night, hoping to fulfill my own God-given destiny.

Though I was hopeful of a bigger purpose being revealed to me, I was terrified of *how* he might decide to use me. He'd left Bethany without an arm. What might he take from me? I worried as a mom because, like most parents, my kids are the world to me. I couldn't imagine something happening to any of them.

So each night I would pray, "Use me, God, as your instrument or however you need me. I'm ready." But that fear would creep into my heart, so I'd throw in, many times, "But don't do that thing you know I can't handle." Just a little prayer clause. I'm sure he understood.

Then, that November, he gave me my first dream. And to make sure I didn't miss his intention, he gave me a second dream.

This time, the dream was with him, God Almighty. I had never had a dream about God before—just want to be clear so you know this wasn't a regular occurrence or think I'm some kind of weirdo Christian or something. Too late?

It was a few weeks after the first one, and in this dream, it was just God's face and him speaking to me. He was a chubby-cheeked Black man with a bright white beard. His beard wasn't filled in, just stubble. I'm not sure how, but in my dream I knew he was God, and he said, "I want you to make this product."

I didn't remember this dream the next morning. It blindsided me later in the day while I was driving my car with my kids. I don't remember where we were going, but as soon as it hit me, the words, "Oh my gosh! I had a dream about God last night!" jumped right out of my mouth.

My kids didn't even look up from their phones. I guess me shouting out that I had a dream with the creator of the universe was not a big deal to them. But since this is their normal response with pretty much anything, it didn't really faze me too much. Except they needed to get this, so I said, "Hello? Did y'all hear me? I had a dream with God in it last night. Isn't that amazing?"

I think one of them feigned excitement and answered, "Yeah, Mom." They didn't know what to think, I'm sure. They were children after all. But even though it was clear they couldn't care less, I kept talking about it, hoping that one of them would actually start listening and be in awe like I was.

"And he wants me to make this *product*," I continued, still dumbfounded.

Still little to no response from the kids, but they were all at least looking at me now. Probably because they knew my tone and that if they didn't pay attention quick, I might go off the deep end. But I could also tell they were gauging me for the look I must give that shows them it's safe to return to their phones. Are cell phones actually taking over our lives? I decided not to try to figure that out on this day. I had bigger things to ponder. Like, why would God care so much about me making this product? What was so special about it? And why me?

Though I had many questions, I didn't try to answer them. I was, however, totally reinvigorated with the idea of pursuing the product.

It was cool for me to have had a dream about God too. And this may sound strange, but all of a sudden, I felt really important. I had been selected. I felt a special kind of pride about it. My first dream already had a spiritual element to it because of *The Dream Giver* and my nightly prayer, but this was confirmation, directly from the dream giver himself.

Normally, I'm a pretty practical and grounded person. I don't have time for profound thoughts or to question things too much. I'm busy… work, kids, all their activities. I pretty much just go and do most days. But this dream gave a whole new depth to my idea. It confirmed for me my belief that my first dream was no accident, and that the idea wasn't really mine. It was something outside of me. Christian, my oldest boy, teasing me one day, said, "You didn't really invent anything, Mom. I mean, it came to you in a dream while you were sleeping." Kids—they'll keep you humble. But I think he was right—I don't believe it came from me, but from God, with an order to fulfill.

I have a lot going on. I can get distracted. I'm sure God knows this about me. He knew he needed to spell it out for me. I don't think he could have made it any clearer though. I mean, actually showing up in my dream and telling me he wanted me to make this product. It would be pretty hard to miss that message, even for me.

I would make it happen.

I think that's always been a thing with me. When I get it into my head that I'm going to do something, I just do it. I'm not known for overthinking things. (It's a blessing and a curse.)

When I was eight years old, I spent almost a year in Valencia, Spain. I was enrolled in an American English school, and during recess I would watch the boys play soccer with my best friend, Heba. I began to fall madly in love—with soccer, not the boys. Unfortunately, the boys wouldn't let the girls play. Occasionally they'd let us play goalie. But I didn't care, I loved it.

When we got back to the States, all I could talk about was soccer. I badgered my parents to get me on a team. It was my first passion, and I played for years in various soccer leagues in Oklahoma City, where I grew up. When I got to high school, however, there wasn't a girls' soccer team, only one for the boys.

This came up one day in Mrs. Koenig's class. We somehow got into a pretty heated discussion about how we needed a girls' team. The boys made the argument: "Where are you going to play? There's only one field and we're using it."

My friend Stephanie was in that class with me, and even though she didn't play soccer, she was just as insulted as I was. What a lame reason not to have a girls' team. We could share the field. Duh. We decided something had to be done. So we stayed behind after class and asked Mrs. Koenig, "What should we do?"

Mrs. Koenig was short, with cropped gray hair and glasses. She heard us out and suggested, "If you feel that strongly about it, you should find out if enough other girls are interested in playing. And then maybe get them all to sign a petition and present it to the school."

That seemed doable to us. We spread the word and found there was interest. Now we needed to secure a classroom where the girls could sign our petition. After school that day, we ran back to Mrs. Koenig, who was just leaving. As she was locking up her room, we asked if we could use her classroom one day that week after school.

She chuckled and said, "No, I'm sorry. I can't stay after school."

Undaunted, we decided to ask our English teacher, Mrs. Null-Miller. She agreed to help us, and the next morning, we made an announcement over the school's PA system for all girls interested in playing soccer to meet up in Mrs. Null-Miller's classroom after school.

It was a success. We got thirty-two names. I took the petition the very next day to the office of the athletic director, Mr. Cook, but only the new football coach, Mr. Pigg (no, I'm not making these names up), was there.

"All these girls are interested in playing soccer," I told him. "We're hoping you will help us start a girls' soccer team."

Mr. Pigg said he would give the list to Mr. Cook.

The next week I went back to follow up on our petition. When I asked Mr. Cook about it, he informed me, in a very matter-of-fact tone, "Oh, it looks like I lost that list."

He lost it?

I turned and left but I didn't cry. At least not till I got home.

That night, I told my dad what happened. He was outraged. He sat me down, his face turning red, but seeming to want to be calm. "This is what you're going to do this time," he said, in a rather scary tone. He then proceeded to give me his advice. "You're going to have another meeting. Then you're going to make several copies of the new list of names. Then you're going to write a letter and you're going to copy everyone on it. The principal, your guidance counselor, Mr. Pigg, Mr. Cook. Everyone you know."

The next day I told Stephanie about what had happened.

"Unbelievable!" she said. "All right, I'm still in. Let's do this."

We went back to Mrs. Null-Miller. It really bothered me to have to ask her again. She had diabetes, and I'd even seen her cry once in class when some kids had made fun of her for rushing out to get some orange juice. She was just so sweet, and I hated to ask for more help from her. Of course, she said yes and stayed after school for us again. She was lovely.

This time only twenty-three girls showed up. It was disappointing, but it was also more than enough for a soccer team.

I did what my dad told me. I typed my letter on his typewriter. (For my future grandchildren, a typewriter is an archaic device once used to write messages. If you made a mistake, you had to start over. There was no "undo" button. If the person this note was intended for was not someone you could just hand it to, you then had to tuck the letter into an envelope, address it, put a stamp on it, and drive to the post office to mail it. Like I said, archaic, but it's important to remember, kids, the struggles mankind once had to simply send a message to someone else. How are you all not better communicators?) I made several copies of it and of our new list and dropped it off to Mr. Cook. He looked at the letter and all the CCs at the bottom, and then at the new list of names on the second page. I was holding my breath, waiting to be dismissed.

He didn't say a word. He just set it on his desk and looked at me. I quietly backed out of the room with a terrified smile on my face, then dropped off my additional copies to everyone else. It was close to the end of the school year, so I figured that was pretty much the end of that.

That September, on back-to-school night, I headed to the cafeteria to get my list of classes. Mr. Cook spotted me. "Did you notice what your seventh period is?" he asked.

I looked down and saw "Intramural Sports." It was soccer. He'd found a soccer coach over the summer. They had hired a new science teacher, who was also going to be the new coach for the boys, too. Now Bishop McGuinness had an official soccer program for both the boys and the girls. It was awesome.

For me, I saw a situation that was unfair that I felt needed to be fixed. And I fixed it. I mean, why wouldn't we have a girls' soccer team? I didn't overthink it. I just did it.

I know God knew that about me. I'm guessing he knew if I felt the world needed a Blinger, that I wouldn't second-guess it. I'd just go make a Blinger. I think he knew he could rely on me, just like he knew he could rely on Bethany Hamilton. He knew she wouldn't be able to stay off her board or stop competing, and then she'd have a beautiful platform to share his message. I believe this book, more than Blinger, is what he intended for me all along. To show what happens when you believe and follow. To share his message with others. With you.

He gives us the gift, the dream. We get to choose to open it or not, and when we arrive to where we're going, we've got to remember and acknowledge who gave it to us. To give him the glory. And he loves long shots. The ones no one expects. This is how others know he must have been involved.

For me, this was the start of four tough years of trying to make it happen—with everything finally falling into place at the very end of the last year. It wasn't easy for me, but I guess in order to have a good book, you need to have a good story, and those don't come from quick and easy. I mean, not many people are that interested in reading about how simple it was for someone to get to the top. There's no story if there's no struggle. This was just the beginning, fortunately, or unfortunately, of a very good story.

CHRISTIAN BUSINESSPEOPLE

Throughout this book you're going to see references to another book, a book that's like a guide on how to do life. It's called the Bible. I never realized before I became a Christian how many amazing life principles are in the Bible. Even business principles that some of the biggest company leaders follow.

If you don't read it for anything else, read it for those reasons. It might help you figure out what's important and what just isn't. And if you do pick it up, start with the second testament. Save the first testament for when you wake up in the middle of the night and need to get back to sleep—it works every time. And don't be mad at me for saying that—my pastor, Larry Redmond, gave me that joke!

Society doesn't usually promote work as a spiritual or even positive endeavor. But according to Scripture, your work and business is very important to God. Over your lifetime you will probably spend more than one hundred thousand hours working. What that time represents, the value and the impact it has, is up to you. You can strive to glorify God in your work ("...whatever you do, do it all for the glory of God," 1 Corinthians 10:31), or you can trade your precious time for money alone. When you work for a higher purpose, the work becomes much better than any currency. It becomes priceless and helps you to lead a more fulfilling life. And God wants that for all of us. Here are some amazing Christian business leaders and companies:

Glyn Bindon—Trijicon

Bob Briner—Roaring Lambs

Larry Burkett—Money Matters

Mark Burnett—Lightworks Media

Charles Butt—H-E-B Grocery

Asa Candler—Coca-Cola

S. Truett Cathy—Chick-Fil-A

Do Wong Chang—Forever 21

Henry Parsons Crowell—Quaker Oats
Peter Daniels—entrepreneur and life coach
Roma Downey—Lightworks Media
Miles Ezell—Purity Dairies
David Green—Hobby Lobby (started in Oklahoma, thank you!)
Henry John Heinz—HJ Heinz Company
R. G. LeTourneau—earthmoving machinery innovator
Tom Love—Love's Travel Stops and Country Stores
(also started in Oklahoma! Woo-hoo!)
Linious McGee—Alaska Air Group
Paul J. Meyer—Success Motivation Institute
Norm Miller—Interstate Batteries
Tom Monaghan—Domino's Pizza
Bud Paxson—Home Shopping Network
Bo Pilgrim—Pilgrim's Pride
Morris Reaves—Cook Out
John D. Rockefeller Sr.—Standard Oil
Anthony Rossi—Tropicana
Lynsi Snyder—In-N-Out Burger
Festus Stacy—Penn Oil
David Steward—World Wide Technologies
Stanley Tam—US Plastic
Hal Taussig—Untours
Sir John Templeton—mutual fund pioneer
Brad Tilden—Alaska Air Group
John Tyson—Tyson Foods
Marion Wade—ServiceMaster
Sam Walton—Walmart
Robert Wegman—Wegmans
Zig Ziglar—author

Chapter 3

"The difference between a successful person and others is not a lack of strength, not a lack of knowledge, but rather a lack of will."

~**Vince Lombardi**, arguably the greatest football coach of all time

If you think of all the million steps it takes to make an idea come true, you probably won't even take the first one. That's why I recommend you try not to think too much, just keep it simple. By keeping it simple, you keep your dream alive, and little by little, you start making it real.

Keeping focused on that one clear goal kept me from overthinking the whole thing and thinking myself right out of doing it altogether.

I hear people thinking and talking themselves out of their dreams all the time. They justify not even trying with a million very logical reasons. That's fine, but I say if you really believe in an idea, stop talking about it and just do it. Don't think about all the things that can go wrong, or all the steps after that. Dumb it down. You don't have to figure everything out now—all you have to do is believe.

❂ ❂ ❂

"Whether you think you can, or you think you can't— you're right."

~**Henry Ford**, founder of Ford Motor Company

In hindsight, I never saw the steps as daunting, probably because I only thought of the main one, which, for most of my journey, was getting a working prototype of my idea.

I knew I needed the prototype, and I knew a few of the other steps I needed to make along the way, because this wasn't my first invention. Don't get me wrong—I never set out to be an "inventor." As a child I wanted to be a forest park ranger, be married to my forest park ranger husband, have lots of kids, and live in the woods where we'd all take care of the animals. As I got older, I didn't know what I wanted to do, which is why I took off for France for a couple of years in my early twenties—not knowing a lick of French, mind you—and then took forever to graduate from college.

I wanted to be a writer for a long time and write that great American novel—hey, maybe that one has finally happened—we'll see what he has planned though, on that.

However, most of my professional life ended up being spent in sales. While I moved back to Europe for a short while after college, where I worked for a tour company in England, most of the rest of my career has been in selling people things I thought they might like to have. I ended up there by happenstance, not by plan, but it turns out I was very good at it.

I probably should have known sales is where I'd end up. When I was in third grade, there was a contest to see who could sell the most magazine subscriptions at my elementary school. The prizes were amazing: huge stuffed animals, pogo sticks, skateboards, books, records, candy.

I knocked on every door in my neighborhood in Edgemere Park all by myself—times were different then. I guess you could say it was my first sales territory. Almost every homeowner in Edgemere, three hundred homes, bought at least one magazine from me. I would ask after the first order, "What about for your husband?" or "Are there any other magazines you'd like?" If no one answered the door, I wrote down on my clipboard their house number under the name of the street I was on (I didn't know how to write an actual address—remember, I was only nine) and kept going back to that house number on that street until I got them.

When I won, by a landslide (surprisingly, no one else had sold anything remotely close to what I had sold), the principal asked which record album I wanted. I said, naturally, "Oh, Meat Loaf: *Bat Out of Hell.*" I did, however, say the word hell as softly as possible. He looked at me wide-eyed, then just laughed as he jotted it down on the prize form.

After graduating from the University of Oklahoma, I decided I was too metropolitan for my home state of Oklahoma. (How many times have I regretted that thought since becoming a mom?) After living in France for a couple years and England for about six months, I chose to go east because I believed it would feel more like Europe than the West Coast.

I took the touring guide experience I'd gotten in England and worked for a small, family-run company in Philadelphia that booked large group tours for universities. After I took the job and moved my dog, Bud, and myself out to Philly, I learned just after my second month had passed that no one lasted more than a couple months in my position—it was essentially a revolving door. They'd hire someone to build leads and establish the contacts—to do the grunt work—then the wife would let them go and the husband would close the deals, keeping all the commissions meant for the sales rep in-house.

I'm a very hard worker. Most employers loved me and my work ethic. So even though I learned of their pattern, I was pretty sure this was not going to happen to me. Ah, to be young and naive again. I had gotten them a trip to Japan with my alma mater, OU, and the money they made on that one trip was more than the salary they were going to pay me for the whole year. I had earned my keep. Plus, I was already in that position longer than the others—going on three months. I was sure I was going to be the exception.

Nope. In my third month, the wife stormed into my office and told me, "You're fired." (Not "We need to let you go." Come on people, have some class!) She then shoved a box into my hands, told me to pack up my stuff, and stormed out.

I had worked really hard on cultivating my contacts and establishing relationships, rapport, and trust with all of them, and this company had just used me and never intended on valuing me long term, though I had moved halfway across the country for the job. I don't really know how I thought to do this in the moment, but while no one was looking, I took the book with all my notes—the goods I knew they wanted—and hid it in the stairwell.

When she came back with my final check and looked through the items I had packed up in my box, I was so nervous. She was short, probably not even five feet tall, but terrifying. You did not want to cross this lady.

I was escorted out into the hallway, and the door slammed shut behind me. The stairwell door was just in front of me, but I was scared she might pop back out at any moment. I started walking toward the elevator. After I'd gone about ten feet without anything else happening, I decided I had to muster up the courage—now or never—and get the binder. I turned around and walked quickly and quietly back to the stairwell, opened the door as softly as possible, grabbed the notebook off the floor, threw it into my box, and flew down the next three flights of stairs. I was sure this woman would have had me arrested if she had caught me with that binder. Once I got out of the building, I started to breathe a little easier.

I know I shouldn't have taken the binder, but I felt the little guy needed a win against these people, and apparently, I was the little guy to do it.

Alone in Philly, not really knowing anyone yet, I was worried. I bought a newspaper and started scouring the job listings. I found one offering $35,000 a year, almost twice the income I had been earning at the travel company, but no experience was required. That sounds about right for me! I called and got an interview set up. During the interview, I told them I didn't have much experience in sales but that I was a quick learner and a hard worker. I was surprised to be hired on the spot with such an increase in pay.

I was going to be trained as a door-to-door meat salesman, and I was thrilled! Yes, I sold meat, door to door. I think a lot of people thought, "Oh, she's from Oklahoma—makes sense."

My sales approach was that I'd go into people's houses and make myself at home, like I was part of the family. If they cursed, I'd curse. If they smoked, I'd pretend to like smoking. If they were quiet and reserved, I did my best to be that way. Today I know that this is an actual sales technique, but back then, I was just trying to fit in and hoping they'd like me. I figured if they liked me, they would buy from me.

I later learned that "mirror and matching" works because it makes people feel comfortable. When you're relatable, it makes people feel good about themselves. If you're a rich, skinny supermodel, no one is relating to you, so you need to tone that part of your life way down. Of course, this wasn't my problem. I was totally relatable.

We did sales training on closing the deal all day in the office. It became almost impossible for customers to say no if you did the close right. We practiced these conversations for hours at a time. Then we'd go out on our sales calls at night. We knew every variation that could possibly happen. It was hard-core *Glengarry Glen Ross* sales training: A-B-C (Always Be Closing).

I'd show up for my appointment, then once inside I'd ask, "Where's the kitchen?"

They'd show me and usually ask back, "Did you bring the steaks?"

That was our call center's hook. We brought either two chicken parmesan entrées or two steak fillets.

I'd look at them like they were crazy for asking such a silly question and say, "Of course I brought the steaks. And I'll even cook 'em for you, if you want."

Once I was in the kitchen, I'd head right to their fridge and start checking out their food. I did this to keep them honest with me and so we could have a legitimate conversation. If they told me they ate one way but didn't, the way I priced it could be too high for their budget, which would mean they wouldn't buy anything, and nobody won. They wouldn't get the service—which the wife probably wanted—nor any of the amazing steaks—which the husband probably wanted. And I wouldn't get the sale—which I definitely wanted or I might not be eating at all.

For some reason, when you open someone's fridge, you immediately become a cherished member of the family. I'm not sure why, but it has to be some universal truth because it was this way every time.

I'd find out how they liked their steaks cooked, and I'd start cooking them dinner. I didn't just say, "Here are your steaks and throw them in the fridge." The sacred fridge. I was creating relationships and forming bonds, and we were having fun. Maybe I didn't always close the deal, but the customers always had a nice time and a good meal.

I took that job thinking I would make $35,000 a year. Little did I know it was straight commissions, which I didn't find out until my third week in, when I didn't get paid.

When I asked where my check was, my boss said, "You didn't sell anything this week."

Dumbfounded, I asked, "What does that have to do with anything?"

It was all good though. I ended up making over $50,000 that year and became their top sales representative. They started hiring more women after me. What was my secret weapon, besides being nice to people? Have fun, be relatable, and feed them.

After that, I did sales for a phone company called Winstar for about three years. I was in the President's Club, winning all the trips and awards. At this time I was reading books on selling to corporations and top officers. I was listening to tapes on selling. Many days after work I'd be the last to leave the office. Everyone got up to go to happy hour at five or five thirty, usually just after our manager left. I did get invited, but most of the time I was like, "Oh, I've got stuff to do. Thanks anyway."

I'd be there sometimes till nine o'clock at night calling companies, and guess who I'd be catching half the time? The CEOs. The top officers. I firmly believe, and tell my kids often, rarely will someone get to the top without a lot of hard work and a strong work ethic. There's a reason people become CEO, and it's not good looks or luck.

My strategy was to go right to the guys who made the decisions. I did my best to skip the gatekeepers, aka the secretaries, who only made closing the deal take longer—sometimes months longer—because they'd push you down to the middlemen and never let you through to the one who called all the shots. You had to find ways around them, and I learned that calling after hours was a great way to get around them, as secretaries don't usually work past closing time (unless they want to get ahead and not be a secretary anymore).

Then came my first invention concept. While at Winstar, I had an idea for a watch that you would use to track and communicate with your kids. It was 1999, and not everyone had cell phones at the time. Definitely not children. It was something adults could rent in an amusement park, or any place really. They could program their phone number into the device, which was designed to be worn on the child's wrist. It was waterproof and could even store a credit card, if the parents wanted. We called it the "Communigator" to make it fun, and it seemed appropriate for all the amusement parks in Florida. We later added an image of an alligator on it.

So I formed my first company and called it Brooks Enterprises Inc. (Brooks was my maiden name.) Later I changed it to BEICOM, because I felt like it was snazzier—more dot com–ish. I raised over $400,000 from friends and family to develop it. I ended up leaving my Winstar job and worked full-time on it. I filed a patent on the idea and eventually had five employees and office space in Alexandria, Virginia. My first start-up.

I was getting pretty far with the Communigator. I had antennae installed in Carowinds amusement park in Charlotte, North Carolina. I had a $2 million contract in the works with a French company that wanted to invest. They had even advanced me $700,000 of it. Unfortunately, the contract process with my lawyers dragged, and the timing ended up not being right. Vision will only get you so far. Unfortunately, or fortunately, timing can be just as big as the idea itself.

On the day the Twin Towers in New York City were attacked in September of 2001, I was in Dallas, Texas, and had a meeting scheduled with Six Flags at their corporate headquarters. I was in my hotel room when my engineer called from his room and told me, "Turn on your TV."

Everyone was in shock. The world stopped. I didn't want it to stop. I was in the midst of making my Communigator dream a reality. I felt helpless. Suddenly I had no control over my business or my plans.

Everything changed that morning, and I didn't know what to do to get it back on track. To this day, I feel guilty that I made those Six Flag employees hold my meeting. They all looked like someone had come in and stolen something very personal from them. I kept trying after that to keep things moving, but there wasn't anything I could really do. I never heard from the French investor again, and of course the remaining $1.3 million didn't come in.

Without faith, life can become pretty scary, pretty fast. We're under the illusion that we're in control, but we're not the ones in charge. I heard once, if you want to make God laugh, make plans. It's hard to understand, even when you believe, why bad things happen. It's not that he allows them to happen—it's that he gave us all free will. We get to choose what we believe, whom or what we follow, how we take care of ourselves, and how we view and treat others. It's this freedom to choose that needs to be grounded in something amazing, something poignant and bigger than ourselves, or we can find ourselves running off the rails.

I had a bit of the advance left, but I was spending over $35,000 a month in employee salaries, engineering consultants, office space, and all the other expenses that go with running a business. I didn't know how long we could last, and no one was investing in anything in the fourth quarter of 2001. It was all very heartbreaking.

That November, I met Dave, my now ex-husband. It was love at first sight. He wanted four kids, I wanted four kids. He wanted his four kids to go to private school, I wanted my four kids to go to private school. We were a perfect match! We were looking at rings within two weeks of meeting each other.

Dave was living and working in Delaware, and I was living just outside of Washington, DC, so he would drive down to see me on the weekends. He loved that I was CEO of my own business, but he knew I was stressing about keeping my employees employed. Especially with Christmas coming, I didn't have the heart to let them go. He believed in me and the product, and he convinced me one night to put the last of my money—all my savings, which was a little over $85,000—into saving my company. Unfortunately, it was like putting a Band-Aid on a gaping wound. Without the influx of the other capital, I couldn't take the next steps to make it succeed. I closed the company just after Christmas.

That dream was over. But thankfully, a new romantic dream was just beginning with Dave.

I took a break from corporate America and started waiting tables. A friend from Winstar saw me and was shocked that I was waitressing, because I had been, like, the top sales rep with them. She told me to call a mutual friend of ours, who offered me a sales job on the spot with a new company, Raindance.

Also around this time, Dave and I got married, and I moved to Delaware.

Though I didn't love my new Raindance job, and I was not the star I had been at Winstar, I was grateful to have it. With Raindance, I was able to work from home, which was helpful because Dave and I had started having babies, one after the other.

Then one day, when my second baby, Christian, was six months old, the owners had everyone on a call to tell us it was all over—they were selling the company and letting us all go. I was floored but not worried. I knew I'd figure something out, as it wasn't a choice really. I was part of a budding family—I had a husband and two babies now—we would do what was necessary to rise to the occasion.

A couple of weeks before this, my mom had started calling me about something called Arbonne. They were headquartered in California but had gotten big in Oklahoma.

When she first told me about it, I was horrified. Arbonne was a network marketing company. I didn't understand multilevel marketing but had heard not-so-great things about it. I was like, "Uh, Mom, I'm not interested in that. I would never do that. I have a good job already, and did you forget I have a college degree? Why are you even talking to me about this?"

I was completely insulted. I was not above selling meat, but lip liners? No way. Even if I had known that a couple of weeks later I was going to need a new job, I still wouldn't have done Arbonne. I was a network marketing snob.

She didn't give up on selling me on it though. And after I lost my Raindance job, she was like, "See? It's a sign. You're supposed to do Arbonne."

She was relentless. One thing that was intriguing to me, however, was how much she loved the products. When it came to products, my mom was the opposite of me. She went to the mall to get her skincare and makeup, not the grocery store, like I did. I found that significant and also weird that she liked them, because they were this no-name brand to me. So her loving them so much was actually a big stamp of approval on their products.

My mom was well-off, so she wasn't asking me to do Arbonne so she could make money off me. She sincerely saw it as something good for me. She was seeing very professional people out in Oklahoma leaving their corporate jobs for Arbonne. When I did more research on the company, I saw there was only one vice president in Delaware, yet hundreds in Oklahoma. I thought everyone in Delaware must hate Arbonne. My second thought was that Delaware's so small, there's probably not room for another VP. But my third thought, which turned out to be the correct one, thankfully, was that maybe the good people of Delaware just hadn't heard of Arbonne yet.

I was still pretty sure it was a scam though. I spoke to a lady my mom referred me to about it. I only agreed to talk to her because I was going to find out everything that was wrong with this Arbonne business and then explain it to my mom so that maybe she would stop bugging me about it. But that call spun me around. I learned that Arbonne was about relationships, networking (of course), and about introducing people to good products—it was just a different way to distribute them. Share products you like with others—like you would a good movie or restaurant—and you get a little commission every time they order. It sounded perfect for a people-loving sales gal like me. I decided to give it a shot and signed on. What did I have to lose?

There are four levels with Arbonne one can achieve. I attained the first level, district manager, as well as qualifying for the second level, area manager, by the end of that first month—basically within twelve days of signing up. By the next month I'd completed the second level and was an area manager. By the end of that summer, four months after starting, I was a regional VP, the third level where you are given a bonus each month if you drive a white Mercedes. My husband and I traded in my worn out mini-van for a brand new Mercedes Benz. It was a whirlwind summer.

This was not the normal pace, mind you, just so I'm not misleading anyone. There was a lot that fell into place that summer for me and my team. We worked hard and I left my little babies to my husband's care many nights, which was shocking to him. The first two nights, he called his mom to come over to help him. By the third night, she told him, "You can take care of your own children." Always loved that she said that! He actually became pretty good at taking care of them too.

When I was in qualification for region and heading into my fourth month, I remember asking him, "If I help with all these events, I'm sure I could make a difference for these women and men on my team, but who is going to watch the kids?"

It was my turn to be in shock when he answered, "I've got the kids. I can give them a bath and put them to bed." I had no idea who he was when he said that. I almost laughed.

So it was an unusually quick journey to the third level with Arbonne. Not the norm, but definitely possible. That was 2006, and ever since, Arbonne has provided an incredible lifestyle for my family that I couldn't be more grateful for.

Along my Arbonne journey, I went nation, the highest level, a month after our third child, Evan, was born. I practically finished that level during contractions. Unfortunately, I lost my nation level in 2008 after the mortgage crisis (but am thankfully still an ERVP). It's turned out to be everything my mom thought it would be for me and more.

Within a few years, even with my successful business, Dave and I started having problems. We did have three children three and under at one point, so maybe that was part of it. We lived in chaos most days, so fighting over stupid things came easy. By 2011 we were separated.

Before my separation, I had started counseling. I had felt I wasn't enough. I wasn't good enough for Dave, for my children, really for the world. I had a lot of personal demons that I was fighting, pretty much since childhood, that had been buried deep but would show up in my life unexpectedly. Didn't matter what I achieved—on the inside I still didn't feel worthy. With the divorce, for my children's sake, I needed to be at my best. Something was missing, and I was about to find out what.

I ended up being paired with the most amazing, caring, and wonderful counselor one could ever hope to have, Jane Galli. During one of our first sessions, I shared with her how I had always wanted to have a relationship with God. She said, "Well then, it's no coincidence why you were paired with me." She has a remarkable relationship with Christ. And she soon became my saving grace during one of the darkest periods of my life. In many ways, she saved my life.

Because of Jane, I was now actively trying to find my faith. I had always wanted to believe, but it just didn't seem to click for me for some reason. I was seeing her at least once a week, usually twice, and she'd let me talk way past our allocated forty-five minutes. And I can talk if you let me. I can talk for hours and never get bored. I may have a talking problem, in fact. Listening, not so good. I try to listen though—just to keep it fair for everyone around me.

I desperately wanted to be a believer. "Fake it till you make it" has worked for me a few times in my life, so I decided to fake my faith until I had it. I started going to church every Sunday. Taking notes. Speaking as if I believed at all my Arbonne events. I was walking the walk, talking the talk. Listening only to Christian radio in my car. Talking to Jane—incessantly. But nothing changed. The outside might have looked different, but the inside was just the same.

Driving one day with my sweet little Evan in the back seat and Christian music playing on the radio, I decided that it wasn't working and wouldn't. I didn't believe it was for me. I needed to move on and accept reality. Believing in God might be for other people, but it wasn't going to be for me. I needed to stop kidding myself. But just as I went to change the radio station, they started sharing a story about a lady in Europe who had won some money but had refused it. She didn't believe it was for her. The same words I had just said in my head played on the radio. I don't remember all of the message, but it struck my heart with a clarity I can't explain and a feeling of love I'd never felt before.

I was saved at precisely the instance I was giving up.

I started bawling, and the Holy Spirit entered me and took over. He told me I was precious. That the gift wasn't just for others, but for me too. And life has never been the same since.

That year, 2012, I found my greatest reward, my faith, during the saddest time of my life, as my divorce was finalized in the courts. Isn't it weird how really bad things can happen in our lives right when really great things are happening? I guess it shouldn't be a surprise though—he is the God of the mountains and the valleys. And when I'm in the valley, that's when I feel the closest to him.

Within six months I was so excited to have found a boyfriend on the dating website Christian Mingle. I fell head over heels. It turned out he was just a Christian who liked to mingle, but before I realized that, I was pregnant with my fourth child, Grace.

Divorced, pregnant, and now heartbroken, I cried every day during that pregnancy. I felt ashamed in church. My belly stuck out like the scarlet letter. I stopped going. Isn't it sad how church can feel like the place where we're most judged? One day, while I was crying and rubbing my tummy, my mom said to me, "Think of it this way—you always wanted four children."

I looked at her in disgust and cried out, "Not like this!" as I continued to rub my belly.

But then Grace was born, and all the sadness was gone. In an instant, it was just pure joy. I went from cursing those delivery nurses out to loving on everybody, especially my new baby girl.

A few weeks later, I saw that the house I'd been looking at in Pennsylvania had come down by almost $100,000, and I pretty much bought it on the spot. By January 2014, my four kids, our dog, Lily, and I moved in, and life was all good again—different, but good.

Like Blinger, had I realized all this was going to happen to me, I don't know how I could have kept going. There was a lot of happiness, but also a lot of pain. Did I want to be divorced from my first love? Or be dumped by the next guy while pregnant with his baby? No. But could I imagine a life without Grace? And not just Grace, but the grace of God that I received. I did have my four children that I always wanted. I was living in a beautiful home. I had a self-sustaining business that was carrying me through so much, where any other job would have fired me long ago. I didn't like some of the journey, but I loved the outcome.

God protects us from seeing all the steps, the future, not to hurt us or keep us in the dark, but so that we don't miss our destiny. If we knew all the hard parts that were to come, we might not ever begin.

The journey is ongoing, and it is never the end, unless you let it be the end. If you're not where you want to be, keep going. It's not over. And it may be that the journey is designed to change you so that you can realize the dream to its fullest.

You don't get there—you *grow* there. You will become the person you need to be along the way. Many times, internal changes need to happen first in order for external things to happen. The journey will naturally grow you into all you need to be when you arrive.

I have a picture frame a friend gave me with a biblical quote on it that I love:

> *"For I know the plans I have for you," says the Lord.*
> *"They are plans for good and not for disaster, to give you*
> *a future and a hope."*
>
> *~**Jeremiah** 29:11*

And under it there's a single word. I never understood the relation between it and the Bible quote until now: journey.

When you believe, you're able to let worry go and trust the path. To trust that your journey is not over, especially when it seems disastrous, and that your future *is* good. You're meant to take the journey that the Lord places on your heart. And grow into your destiny with faith in his will for your life.

ANGIE'S TOP TEN TIPS FOR SUCCESS

1. **Be ethical.** Don't lie, cheat, or swindle. Make integrity the foundation of your business. It doesn't mean you can't be ornery, but guard your integrity—it's everything.

2. **Be yourself.** You were created for great things—your own great things. Your journey is like your fingerprint: it's completely unique to you. Be real. Be you.

3. **Be kind to everyone.** Always. View everyone with a sign on their forehead that reads "I want to know I matter." Show them they matter.

4. **When you hit a wall, don't stop or waste energy trying to understand why.** It will all make sense in the end. Here are my recommended three options when you hit a wall:

   - **Find a way around it.** Go over, go around, go under.

   - **Find another route.** There may be a different path to get to your goal. Open your mind, consider your options, and be open to changing your course.

   - **Find the strength to start over.** Sometimes the only way is to turn around and start again. Head back to square one and rebuild. I've had to do that more than once on my Blinger journey!

5. **Put pride in your back pocket.** Pride could be your unraveling if you don't put it aside. What other people think of you doesn't matter and is really none of your business.

6. **Take a break.** When you feel stuck, it's okay to take a step back to get some distance and breathing room. It can't last long, however. I'd say a week, tops. In Arbonne it was twenty-four hours. Focus on other important priorities in your life and then get back to work.

7. **Give your goal a bigger meaning.** You can't be in it just for the money or fame. These are shallow and can be unfulfilling. Many times, they are also only temporary. If you don't have a bigger meaning, find one. Make it life changing.

8. **Don't quit.** Never see quitting as an option, no matter what. Find a way to keep moving forward (or sideways or backward). Just keep moving.

9. **Be careful whom you listen to.** Many people will give you advice, but only a few will know what they're talking about. Trust your gut and follow wisely.

10. **Enjoy the journey and trust the process.** It may be a long one after all. You may look nuts to everyone else too, so might as well keep joy in your heart. Take your business seriously, but not yourself. Laugh at how crazy you feel sometimes and then just keep committing to the pursuit. Success will come. Believe.

Chapter 4

"Never be afraid to trust an unknown future to a known God."

~**Corrie ten Boom**, author of *The Hiding Place*
who helped many Jews escape from the Nazis
during the Holocaust in World War II by hiding
them in her home

I hear this question a lot now: "How did you do it?" I have tried to answer it again and again, but most people don't seem to have the three hours needed to hear my response. (It's really a loaded question for me.) So, I thought, if I wrote a book on what happened, I could just say, "Oh, it's all in my book, just read my book. In fact, you can have it for free—I have a hundred copies in my trunk!" Then we could both move on with our lives.

But now, as I'm writing and rewriting and thinking about it all, I'm not sure my book will have all the answers. Mainly because everyone's journey is going to be different. We all have different experiences, talents, connections, strengths (and weaknesses) to discover and figure out along the way. What I can tell you is that you're going to have to be okay with not having all the answers. You're going to have to dive into the places you don't understand and learn how to swim while in the water. However, since I believe my mission is to help you, and since you didn't put my book down during the introduction when I told you "you need to be prepared to work hard"—because let's face it, that's how you do it—I will continue.

When I first had my dream, because of my first start-up, I knew I had to take steps to protect my concept. I was going to be talking to a lot of people, and I had to do what I could to protect my idea as much as possible. Before I shared my idea with any engineers or anyone else I would need in order to develop it, I knew I first had to have a nondisclosure agreement (NDA).

If you have an original idea and you're ready to forge ahead, find a good patent and trademark lawyer who can write up the appropriate NDA. My attorney, Glenn Massina, is literally the best patent and trademark lawyer out there. He's saved me many times over the years, so I'd recommend him. Plus he's a great guy. He works in Pennsylvania. Look him up!

Ideally, you want to hire a lawyer, get a good NDA, and incorporate before you begin. I didn't take any of these steps at first. I was being frugal, since I only had about $15,000 in my 401(k) to invest. I figured I needed all that to pay an engineer to get a prototype developed. I found my old NDA from BEICOM and updated it with my new concept, current address, and the year.

By this time, I had decided to call my device Blinger. A hairstylist friend of mine, after I described the idea to her, said "Oh, like a blinger." And that was it.

With a product name and an NDA ready, now I just needed an engineer. I learned from Google that I needed a mechanical engineer. And then I learned about these sites that pair inventors with engineers—the dreamers with the people who make the dreams a reality. There are many of them. The one I used was Elance (later called Upwork). I believed having a prototype made of my idea would not only validate it was possible, but also allow me to demonstrate my vision and raise funds for the next steps. I signed up with Elance and posted my job:

> **BLINGER • Mechanical Engineering**
> *We're interested in developing a handheld plastic applicator that will apply gems to different surfaces. Please sign NDA if interested. Once we have your NDA, we will send more details so that you may bid on the job.*

WHAT IS AN NDA, AND WHY DO I NEED IT?

A nondisclosure agreement (NDA) is a document that basically says those who sign it won't share any part of your idea with anyone else. You'll want this agreement to be signed by everyone—employees, engineers, business associates, even friends. Everyone you share your idea with should sign your NDA.

Your NDA should include that your intellectual property (IP) is also protected. Your IP is anything conceptualized or developed by you, your employees, or hired consultants. You don't want them trying to claim that the outcome of the work you paid them to do in any way belongs to them. A nondisclosure and intellectual property agreement is a more robust NDA and states that the work being developed will belong to your company in the end (and not that they'll just keep your idea confidential).

Your NDA should include:

- **Time frame.** I recommend five years. If you're looking to license your product, however, some companies won't sign one for that long. Reduce the period to three years if you need in those instances, but don't go below three years. I didn't get to a successful place in my business until the end of my fourth year, which isn't uncommon, so I highly recommend you make it for five years whenever possible.
- **The nature of the confidential information.**
- **What isn't confidential about the information.**
- **Details about everyone involved in the contract.** This essentially means that you name everyone who's party to the contract and include pertinent details, such as titles and addresses.

While these points above are pretty common in all NDAs, different business ideas will have different requirements. Speak to your attorney to make sure your NDA is right for your idea.

Within an hour, several interested engineers had signed and sent back my NDA. After I shared more details of what I was looking to create with the first few engineers, I started getting good questions back on what exactly I wanted. This was the beginning of my specifications list. Their questions led me to fleshing out the idea further, and so as I spoke to more and more engineers, I naturally became clearer on what I needed from the potential candidates. One of the things I discovered about engineers is that they love to share their know-how, so I just soaked it all up. I became increasingly more knowledgeable about my product until, eventually, I was *the* expert on it. Which is how it should be.

I think it's important to understand that I knew literally nothing about mechanical engineering, making a plastic device, or manufacturing a product like this, but I moved ahead anyway. I want you to get this because I think for many people, to do something you have zero knowledge about is scary and even a deal breaker. No one wants to look dumb. I get that. I just want you to know, it's okay to *not* know. It's normal not to know too much in the beginning about what you're developing. Your knowledge will grow with every step you take. Be confident in that. You will become the smartest one in the room about your idea if you keep going. Listen and learn and never be afraid to ask questions. Take your pride and put it to the side. Imagine how proud you'll be when it all becomes real. Focus on *that* prideful moment if you need to, and let these early ones go.

Also know that you can't do many things alone. You're going to have to bring others in and trust often. Strangely, no one stole my idea in the four years it took to make it. I think it's like many ideas—others don't always see it. I'm not saying you're safe, but in reality most people are working on and worried about their own things. Recently, when I shared how much we sold with someone, she responded, in shock, "For hair stickers?" I tried to act like I wasn't insulted.

But that's the point too. Not everyone will get your idea or what's so great about it. That's okay. That may protect you. As long as you believe in it, that's all that matters. Remember you have the clear vision; it was given to you. Your job is to figure out how to get others to see it, but just know not everyone will and that will only help you to learn how to draw the picture more clearly. The right ones will see it when you're ready.

Soon I could gauge the potential candidate's knowledge to an extent, or at a minimum I knew if they were thinking it through. I'd say there are a few engineers and talented factory men and women in China that probably know my product better than me now, but I had to become that person first.

I asked all the engineers I spoke with to submit a rough idea of the design they had in mind, a time frame to develop it, and how much it would cost.

In general, you want to work with people you find easy to work with and who are willing to invest a little time to win your business. The smart ones cover those costs in their proposal, and if they don't get the gig, the time spent on the proposal is just the cost of doing business. This is entrepreneurial thinking, by the way.

Entrepreneurs, like salespeople, know that they're not going to win them all. Some will just be a time or money loss at the end of the year. That's part of the risk of being in business for yourself.

As an entrepreneur, you're not working for the weekly paycheck—you're working for the check you're going to get three years from now, or five. That's your big-picture focus. It's not a quick race around the track; it's more about endurance. It's a cross-country race—and I mean the whole country.

You have to be able to imagine working for years before you receive any money in return. To even be paying employees that you need in order to make it happen before you get paid. They're the employee; you're the entrepreneur. They have to be paid; you have to wait until the company you're building can afford to pay you. You cannot work like an employee and an entrepreneur. Pick one. You can't operate under both mindsets.

And your start-up could also never pay you. Failure and success both could be a reality—look at my first start-up, BEICOM—some successes, but in the end, it failed. But I grew from it and I learned, and it prepared me for Blinger—so it's a part of the overall journey and the eventual success that's now happened. So was BEICOM really a failure if it helped me succeed with Blinger?

Fear, doubt, complaining, laziness, excuses are not part of an entrepreneurial mindset. Get rid of them. They don't serve you.

I've heard that the biggest regrets people have at the end of their lives are not the things they did, but the things they didn't do. So though this sounds hard and a lot will be, it will most likely be worth it in the end. Don't be afraid of being an entrepreneur—be afraid of regretting not being one.

We all know the risks it takes to get there. And this is why I think we all love when a start-up, the underdog, makes it. The battles are real, but so are the rewards. A modern maxim says, "People tend to overestimate what can be done in one year and to underestimate what can be done in five or ten years." Set your mindset appropriately from the beginning and it will keep you from expecting too much, too soon, from too little work.

Here are some of the early designs that came in for Blinger.

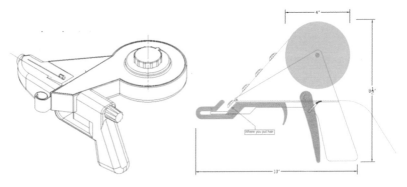

Gun-shaped concept designs.

I decided to reject both right away, because it soon occurred to me that most people probably wouldn't like the idea of holding up a gun-shaped device to their heads.

One of the first engineers I spoke to said there was no way I could get my concept developed on my own and that he wasn't interested. That bothered me for a little while, but then I just had to let it go. Not that his words could have stopped me. If anything, I usually get fired up when someone says I can't do something (just to prove them wrong, I guess).

Don't let anyone tell you what you can and cannot do. I mean, look, he was clearly wrong. Though it did take me a while to make Blinger a viable product, much longer than I thought or wanted, his words didn't stop me from pursuing what I knew I could do. Which makes me think of this great quote from *Bee Movie*:

> *"According to all known laws of aviation, there is no way that a bee should be able to fly. Its wings are too small to get its fat little body off the ground. The bee, of course, flies anyway. Because bees don't care what humans think is impossible."*

I love this. I mean, how could anyone know what you're capable of accomplishing or have the impudence to think they know? You're the only one who can determine your limits. Others should never get a vote on that.

And those who do know you? They can be even more negative when you're attempting to do something different. They know your history and possibly even your past failures. But those prior mistakes may be exactly what you needed to happen in your life in order to be successful now.

My recommendation is don't let anyone determine your destiny. Only God knows your future. And if you believe in him, then you know he gets the deciding vote. "He who is in you is greater than he who is in the world." (1 John 4:4).

So yes, in addition to that first engineer, there would be many more obstacles and naysayers in my way. The proverbial bullies and giants in *The Dream Giver*. But, with God's help and my own stubborn nature, I was going to overcome them all—I was even going to have to overcome a literal plague from the Bible. Not locusts. Not frogs. Not hail. I wish.

Chapter 5

"Anyone who thinks that they are too small to make a difference has never tried to fall asleep with a mosquito in the room."

~**Christie Todd Whitman**, fiftieth Governor of New Jersey

I ended up not hiring any of the engineers I had been speaking with at that time, because in January of 2015, I discovered that I and all four of my beautiful, precious children had...wait for it...lice! Oh, the joys of motherhood. The "dry scalp" I had been experiencing all winter was not actually dry scalp at all.

As you can imagine (or worse, have experienced), life as I knew it came to an abrupt halt. Nothing else mattered. We spent the next two months doing every remedy known to man, to only end up spending hundreds of dollars at a lice treatment center (yes, these exist—you would have no reason to know this until you have a reason to know this).

Lice do not jump. They crawl from head to head. And they are apparently now conquering the world, as we learned there's such a thing as "super lice," which you can't get rid of with anything you buy at the store. They can survive the chemicals—don't believe otherwise. The only thing that works is the nit comb. Don't cover your children's heads in mayonnaise, please. You literally have to comb the little critters and their little baby egg sacks that they stick on your hair (I know, the irony) out every few days, or whatever the life cycle is (I choose to forget), until they're no longer living on your head surviving off your blood and skin. They don't go to animals. They don't go to other hairy parts of the body. (Apparently our heads are the constant perfect temperature for them to survive.) I cringe even writing this and now, all of a sudden, I itch everywhere.

In any case, I'm rushing to get through this part of the story, which I include only so you don't think I was a total slacker for these two or three months (when my life was traumatized) or a horrible Christian for not listening to God when he told me to make this product.

Nope. A little, tiny bug stopped me in my tracks. Lice conquered me and my children that winter, and I've still not fully recovered.

Thankfully, by the spring of 2015, we were lice-free.

Throughout these months, I was a little frustrated about being side-tracked from my journey, but I have learned along the way that delays were generally his way of protecting me, maybe from hiring the person who would have gotten the project right. Yes, I said "right." Because if the first engineer I had hired had produced this darling product and everything worked out just perfect right out of the gate, then where's the story in that? How dull. And I would have missed out on so much... people whom I know and love now and experiences that I grew from and that I love to share with others. My journey and my growth would have been stunted.

One afternoon that March, my mom, children, and I went to see Disney's live-action remake of *Cinderella*. This movie turned out to become just the spark (more like firecracker) I needed to get my focus back on track for Blinger.

About halfway through the movie, when Lily James enters the ballroom, I wanted to throw up. Not because of Lily James, of course, because she's like the most adorable person ever. But because of what was in her hair. It wasn't lice. Ha-ha! It was much worse.

She had hundreds of Swarovski crystals in her hair. They were beautiful. And I was sick.

Here I was with this idea I'd had for months. I even had a dream where God told me to make this product, and what did I do? Basically nothing.

And now it was clearly all over. Someone had invented a device that put crystals in the hair.

I sank down in my seat and almost cried. If my kids hadn't been there and it wouldn't have disrupted their enjoyment of the film, I think I would have.

I let myself down. Worse, I let him down. I had asked him for my destiny. He'd given it to me. And I fumbled it.

When I got home, I decided to look up how they did it. I remember feeling so curious (and a tiny bit jealous, which I think is the absolute worst emotion one could ever have) about the person who had come up with the solution. I was dying to see what it looked like. How they designed it and how it worked. And of course I was going to buy it, because I still wanted one for my girls and me.

That's when I learned that the costume designer for the movie, Sandy Powell, had glued hundreds of Swarovski crystals onto Lily's and Helena Bonham Carter's hairpieces (probably because the adhesive wasn't safe for actual hair) *by hand*. She had spent hours gluing them and placing them, one by one.

I was elated! We were back in business.

They clearly could have used a Blinger. Not to mention stones with hair-safe adhesive. I wonder what Sandy Powell would have done with all those hours she lost on those wigs if she could have them back?

It was official. The world needed my device. At least Hollywood did. Whoever needed it, he wanted it done, and I still hadn't let him down. I was reenergized. After *Cinderella*, I was on a mission—an unstoppable one.

Chapter 6

"There are 106 miles to Chicago. We have a full tank of gas, half a pack of cigarettes, it's dark, and we're wearing sunglasses. Hit it!"

~Jake and Elwood Blues, *The Blues Brothers*

Some people never pursue their dreams. They *think* a lot about every little step but don't actually *do* many of them. They spend more time thinking than doing. Or they get the steps out of order of priority and do the ones that don't really matter. The ones that should come later or are simply easier to do. Here's a tip: the real work, the stuff that moves you forward, is almost never the easy work. It is usually the hard work, the least fun work, and sometimes the scary work. If it's not any of those, it's probably a waste of your time, and worse, it's a trick of the mind that you're growing your business when in actuality you're not.

Many people I recruited for Arbonne were like this. They were ready to quit after just a few months, sometimes weeks, sometimes the day after they signed up, because they didn't see any quick success, or because *one* person said no to them, or because—the biggest reason—they no longer believed it was possible. And of course, it is possible, because there are thousands of hugely successful Arbonne consultants who have reached the highest levels. Here's another tip: if one person has done it, then that means it's possible for someone else to do it. It's that simple. Abraham Lincoln said it this way: "That some achieve great success is proof to all that others can achieve it as well."

Many of these consultants would get caught up on things that didn't really matter, that didn't move the ball forward, and it prevented them from seeing any real progress—though they felt like they were working. It's sort of like dribbling on the soccer field just for the sake of dribbling. Showing off, but ultimately with nothing to show for it. The point is not how fancy the footwork is. It's moving the ball down the field and getting it in the back of the net. With Arbonne, this is asking people to buy your products and to join your business. That's it. It's pretty much the only work that matters in the beginning. Once you were good at that, then you could, and should, add on the work of passing that knowledge forward by training others on how to do those two things.

They would come up with every reason why Arbonne was not working for them, and how it wouldn't work, instead of just *doing* the work. I came to learn that there are three mindsets: blaming, justifying, and building.

- *Blaming*—when they'd say how if only Arbonne had deodorant (we have this now, y'all can't say this anymore!) or toothpaste or if only so-and-so would train them on this, then they could be successful. They blamed their lack of success on everything and everyone else.

- **Justifying**—missing or canceling events, or just quitting because they had something come up with their children, spouse, or schedule, or they'd say how they were actually not really interested in being an RVP, making a corporate income while working from home and getting a Mercedes. (Bah! Who needs a free one of those?)

- **Building**—*the* mindset. A no-matter-what attitude. Doing the work that's hard and/or scares you over and over, daily, until you've reached your goal. And, bonus, it no longer scares you.

You can only have one of these mindsets operating at a time. It's impossible to build if you're blaming or justifying. Same with your start-up. You're either doing it or you're not. There is no gray area. Building takes heart and courage to do, especially when it's tough. Identify what it takes to make a living at what you're dreaming to do. Then strengthen your character by only doing that work in the beginning.

I also see people wasting a lot of time—and money—on image. They make business cards, rent fancy office space, design darling logos, show up to every meeting, and take lots of notes. Smiling, asking great questions. But none of that matters unless they're doing the key work that's moving them toward the key goals. If you want to know if you're spending your time and money in the right place, ask yourself this: Will this item or work generate income or, depending on the business, attract investors? If the answer is not a resounding yes, then it's a waste of time, effort, and probably money.

I didn't incorporate or hire my lawyer until I *had* to do those things. I didn't have business cards made until 2018, because I didn't need or want to spend time or money on that when I could just tell people my phone number or give them my email. (I only made business cards when I went to Dallas Toy Fair for the first time—four years after my dream, and after I had a manufactured product that I could sell.) It's okay if you want to design a logo and make business cards. I'm just saying that this is not going to entice an investor. They won't care about your logo because they're probably going to want to change the name of your product anyway, so it's a waste of time and money—in my opinion.

Do the right work first, then make yourself look good and professional, and then ideally reap the rewards. Focus on the thing that matters most to get your business off the ground. This is important to figure out right away.

I believed if people could see Blinger in action, if they could have the experience of it, like I had seen and felt in my dream, that they would not only get it, but they would be excited about it. And now I know that's right. Even today when I tell people about my product, I can tell they don't really get it. It's only when I pull it out of my purse and apply five stones to my hair in three seconds flat—that's when I see them getting it.

I knew early on I needed a simple device that I could use just to show people how fun it would be to place sparkly crystals in their hair wherever they wanted. I felt if I could do that, girls and women would love it. And let's face it: if a woman likes something that makes her feel pretty, she'll buy it.

As I said, I would be right about this eventually, but now, in the early summer of 2015, more than six months after I had my dreams, what I needed was to listen to my own advice here and get an engineer on board to develop a working prototype.

It seems like a simple product when you see it now, but it wasn't simple to most of the engineers I hired.

The first working prototype for Blinger had about eighteen plastic parts, and that wasn't even counting all the screws, springs, and other nonplastic parts. There were forty-four parts in all. What I learned though, is the plastic parts were the ones that mattered the most. The quantity and size of those pieces will dictate everything in the end—your business's economic model hinges on understanding this.

The plastic parts are what make your device unique and also determine your core costs for your product. Each plastic piece requires its own mold to be created, and then all the molded pieces come together to make up the device as a whole. All the molds represent the tool that must be built to manufacture your product. For a long time I thought the tool was the expensive part—and it can be, initially—but it's the price per plastic part that *keeps* costing you. That's the cost that affects your price point at retail. So it's important that all these add up to make sense for the retailer and the consumer.

The first firm I hired, let's call them Firm 1, made some great drawings of several potential designs, and they did make a nonworking solid plastic model from one of the drawings we selected that I fell in love with, but they never made it into an actual functioning prototype.

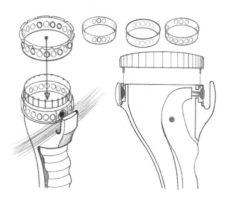 

Concept drawing of first Blinger.   *CAD rendering of Blinger, July 2015.*

I made two major mistakes in hiring this firm: the first was that they were located in Europe, which created several issues, the time difference among them. The second was that Firm 1 was a one-man show. He was an older man, probably in his late sixties, with a young daughter (for his age), and he was divorced. I think I felt a kinship to him, being a single parent myself. Or maybe because of his age, I felt I could trust him.

The problem when you work with a lone guy is that it's just them on the job. If other jobs are happening, or someone is paying them more, your job might be low on the priority list. The problem with hiring someone outside your own country is, if things start to go south, it can be hard to fix from the other side of the world and the legal fees could break you.

Of course, I didn't know these were mistakes at the time, and my relationship with Firm 1 started off great. I decided to not hire him on his full proposal, trying to be smart and careful with my limited funds, and signed him just for the first step: creating renderings of different design concepts. He provided several possible versions of my product in a very timely manner. Then he went through each design, discussing the pros and cons, and together we selected one of the drawings.

I enjoyed that experience. I felt it was professional and simple, so I hired him for the next step, which was actually creating the engineering files of that design that could be used to make the prototype.

However, as time went on, I started to notice him getting angry easily. He also started interjecting himself into other aspects of my business, which I didn't like. I wanted him to design the product, do his thing, and let me worry about the rest.

It was kind of my fault initially though, because I went to him with several questions about manufacturing and costs. I did this because I discovered that *Shark Tank* was holding auditions in Maine at the end of July, and I decided I had to be there. But in order to audition I had to prepare a business plan. I wanted to get everything in my business plan as close to accurate as I could so I could make a strong presentation.

I don't put a lot of stock in business plans this early in the game or spending time on them until I'm much farther along, but sometimes we can't get farther along without them. I do believe in trying to talk to people who know about money and business, like investors, because you learn so much when you do. And they always want to see your plan, so I had to do it, even though I felt it was premature. Getting an audition for *Shark Tank* was not an opportunity I wanted to pass up. I needed manufacturing cost-type information in order to write the plan.

Therefore, I reached out to Firm 1 with my questions, which only he would have the possible experience to answer, and I think that made him feel like he needed to be more in charge. Don't get me wrong, he was a smart guy, but I was paying him to create a design, not be the chief financial officer, and worse, he was getting negative and questioning my reasoning on every call or email now. Instead of doing the job I hired him to do, he was distracted with mine.

Of course, there are times when the details matter. But when perfection and minutia are overly explored, people can get stuck. Caught in the weeds of what-ifs. To me, we were wasting time obsessing about numbers when we didn't even have a product. I needed information, yes, but I didn't need it to be exact—at least not till we had a working prototype. I needed to prove the concept first—that this product could be made and work as intended. Logically, how could we have a discussion about relevant manufacturing numbers and costs when we didn't even know how many plastic parts the device would have?

I suggested that he not get caught up on this. "Let's make the best use of our time and money and get the prototype figured out first," I said. "Then we can figure out actual costs and projections."

Ultimately, I realized it was time to part ways. Unfortunately, he made me pay him thousands of dollars before he would send the engineering work he'd done. He ended up taking half my savings. Plus, the CAD design files that he sent, which I couldn't open and verify because I didn't have the right software, were not actual engineered design files. But it was too late when I discovered that. He had my money, and to sue him overseas was a small fortune. I had to move on and let it go.

So aside from making a nonworking plastic model, Firm 1 and I never really got off the ground. And because of some bad timing, the plastic model was going to arrive a day too late for me to bring to the *Shark Tank* audition. Forget about being eaten alive by the Sharks— without a 3-D rendering of my idea, I wasn't sure if I could even get inside the Tank.

LEARN FROM MY MISTAKES

Here are some things I learned the hard way from working with Firm 1. Hopefully I can spare you some of these headaches.

- **Don't hire people outside your country.** You should hire people that live in your own country whenever possible. When Firm 1 and I had a dispute, there was really no way to pursue him legally—it was too expensive. You can find amazing people in your own country to work with and should stay local whenever possible.

- **Don't pay for files (or any goods) until you've verified they're what they're supposed to be.** Duh. I trusted him because he seemed like a sweet older man. I lost thousands of dollars (for these fake files that he sent as the "work") and months in time.

- **Verify credentials.** I later realized that Firm 1 wasn't even an engineer. He had a degree in design and art. No wonder his drawings were so good. Ask where they went to school. I assumed when my job post requested a mechanical engineer, only mechanical engineers would apply.

- **Get references.** If you ask clear and direct questions of a reference and they give you an indirect answer, that's a warning sign. Pursue that. Eventually they'll probably come clean and tell you what they really think. I've found getting references can be a great way to discover the problems with your candidates. No one's perfect, so ask your reference not only what they liked about your candidate but what they wish had been a little better too. Only you can decide what you can live with and what's going to be a deal breaker.

- **If you go through Upwork or another third party, don't go off that platform to work with the engineers directly.** The third party will hold your money in escrow and you'll get support from them, should there be any discrepancies with the work.

Chapter 7

"A person has to remember that the road to success is always under construction. You have to get that through your head. That it is not easy becoming successful."

~**Steve Harvey**, famous comedian and author of many books, including *Act Like a Success, Think Like a Success*

Before heading to Maine to try out for *Shark Tank*, I formed a new business entity for Blinger. This was to protect my Arbonne business from being commingled with my Blinger business, and it was also required on the application.

I named my company GEMC^2, after my children and me: G for Grace, E for Evan, M for Mom, and two Cs (or C squared) for Cambria and Christian. I thought it was cute and kind of cool because it has the word *gem* in it, and also "EMC^2," which seemed *very* smart.

Speaking of the theory of relativity, did you know this came to Einstein in a dream? Also inspired by dreams: the sewing machine (Elias Howe); the structure of DNA (Nobel Prize–winner Dr. James Watson); Google (you know who did this, if not, it's easy to look up!); the periodic table of the elements (Dmitri Mendeleev); the structure of the atom (Niels Bohr); Mary Shelley's *Frankenstein* (the world's first horror novel, and if you haven't read it, I recommend it—it's much better than the movie!); and now, Blinger (Angie Cella)—another amazing contribution to society.

They say all of your brain is "alive" when you're dreaming, not just one part of it, and that you store everything you've ever learned in your prefrontal cortex. So, while you're sleeping, your mind can hypothesize and essentially test theories out. Like a scientist.

I remember reading a book in college about this village that took dreams very seriously, and the villagers would attempt to make or recreate their dreams, even the children's, almost every day. Dreams ruled their culture.

I think if you start to pay attention and make dreaming a little more purposeful, you'd be surprised at what connections begin happening. If anything, you'll have a greater sense of creativity.

SETTING UP YOUR BUSINESS ENTITY

Here's a quick breakdown of common types of businesses.

- **Sole proprietorship:** only you and created using your Social Security number.
- **Partnership:** you and one or several others—a situation where you all cover costs and divide profits together.
- **Corporation** (including C-Corp and S-Corp): a company or group of people authorized to work together to run the business.
- **LLC:** a company that combines aspects of sole proprietorships, partnerships, and corporations, with limited risks to the owners.

When I set up my business for Blinger, I chose to make it an LLC. Some think a corporation is best. They say you're more protected personally if you're ever sued, but I was told both are safe. If you plan on having investors, having a corporation is better, however I chose an LLC because my accountant said the tax liabilities would be less in the beginning. Whatever you decide, you can always change it later. Talk to an accountant and a lawyer to determine what's best for you.

I wanted to be ready for anything that might happen at the audition. I spent a few weeks preparing my business plan. Thankfully I knew quite a bit about business plans from BEICOM. I had some impressive wording in there too, much of which was done by a former employee, David Thayer. He was brilliant. A Wharton undergrad in economics, MBA in economics and operations from University of Chicago Booth School, and then another master's in international history from the London School of Economics. Besides all that, David is just a genuinely nice guy.

Anyway, one quick tip from my BEICOM days: don't be afraid to hire people smarter than you. They'll make you look smart.

We packed up the car, and I drove to Maine with my mom and kids to where the *Shark Tank* auditions were being held. This was technically a work thing, but my kids are like body parts for me; they just pretty much go where I go, and I've found, most of the time, I don't function well without them—like *actual* body parts. Besides, it was summer. I wanted us to explore. Visit some lighthouses and rocky coastline. Grab some cute pictures of the kids eating lobster. I turned it into a mini vacation.

To me, it's all an adventure. You know, life. And when you're a work-from-home parent, work and the kids are all intertwined. In Arbonne we talked about this a lot, because to build that business, you must weave it into the nooks and crannies of your life. Your life keeps going after you sign up. You can't just stop everything because you need to make a call. You don't get the luxury of going to an office and not having any interruptions from your kids while you work. You're changing a diaper while you're talking to a customer. You're kissing boo-boos and drying tears, or holding them on your lap while typing up an email that needed to go out two days ago. You're working while you're dealing with it all. The boundaries are definitely blurred.

Have you seen the movie *Body of Lies* with Russell Crowe, who plays a CIA veteran running an undercover operation from the US to take out terrorists? There's a scene where he's on the phone with Leonardo DiCaprio, who's in Jordan, while he's helping his little boy use the potty. He's shouting into the phone, "Blow up the target already!" (or something like that). That's what it's like to be a work-from-home parent. Well, mostly.

CREATING A BUSINESS PLAN

A business plan is a detailed document of what your product or service idea is, why people need it and would spend money for it, how you're going to market it, revenue potential, etc. It's intense. According to SBA.gov, any business plan should include the following sections:

- **Executive summary**—a snapshot of your business.
- **Company description**—describes what your company intends to do.
- **Market analysis**—shows that you did your homework and that your idea isn't just a whim. You provide research on your industry, market, and competitors.
- **Organization and management**—outlines your business and management structure.
- **Service or product**—describes the products or services your business will be offering.
- **Marketing and sales**—talks about how you'll market your business and shares your sales strategy.
- **Funding request**—assesses how much money you'll need to keep your business operational for the next three to five years.
- **Financial projections**—essentially balance sheets that show potential income and costs.

A business plan is a lot of work, and it's a work always in progress. You will constantly update your business plan as your business evolves. If you're looking for investors in your business or intend to secure a business loan, you're going to need it.

EXECUTIVE SUMMARY

Management Team:
Angie Cella – Founder and President

Currently Personally Invested:
$95,000

Pre-Money Valuation:
$1,000,000

Angel Investment Goal: $250K

Use of Funds:
- Manufacturing
  - Blinger Tool
  - Strip Tool
- Marketing
- Initial Production Runs

Business Description: Blinger™ is a device that applies Swarovski® crystals, pearls, rhinestones, or other gems to the hair without heat or electricity.

Market Need: There is currently not a device on the market that applies crystals to the hair. Yet there is a large market desiring this trendy and stylish look for prom, weddings, black-tie events, New Year's Eve, 4th of July or just for fun. This will be a new hair tool in a unique and new segment of the hair and beauty market. Celebrities such as Hayden Panetierre, Paula Abdul and Bella Thorne have all applied gems to their hair. In Disney's Cinderella (2015), Lilly James and Helena Bonham-Carter had Swarovski® crystals throughout their hair.

Our Solution: Blinger™ gives females of all ages the ability to create these desired hair styles more easily and with much more versatility. The bottom side of the crystals are coated with a special adhesive that is specifically designed for hair (and skin). This makes the application and removal of the crystals safe for hair. Plus, using only Swarovski® means we are using the most beautiful, brilliant and safest crystals in the world. Blinger™ applies the crystals without heat, batteries, or electricity. Our customers load our specifically designed strips into their Blinger™ to apply crystals to their hair – they place a section of hair into the notch, squeeze the handle and a beautiful crystal is applied. To remove the crystals, they simply brush them out.

Target Markets: Initially we're focusing on the consumer market thru our e-commerce website. Blinger™ could be sold in hair salons, dance studios, to gymnastic teams, ballroom dancers, craft stores as well as through small and big box retailers such as Ulta, Swarovski® stores, Claires, Wal-Mart, Target, etc.

Competition: There are a few companies marketing 'gems' for hair but there is not any company that has a device that applies gems to the hair. In addition, all competitors have a few if not several drawbacks, either by requiring electricity or needing heat or batteries, are difficult to apply and/or remove the gems, expensive for the type of gem they're receiving (basically with very little sparkle affect), do not market or attract adult women or would be too difficult or too expensive for children, and last and most important of all, many are damaging to the hair – this is oddly especially true for the products geared towards children.

Key Assumptions: [What do you assume about your product?]

Key Dynamics: Blinger™ breaks even quickly – estimated within less than a year. Our model is a high-margin business, a relatively "light" model that produces a cost-efficient, high-cash, scalable business. In the aggregate, both revenue and net profit grow rapidly, enabling us to break even quickly. [JUST COPY WHAT I WROTE HERE! Lol]

Key Statistics: Year one growth reflects, with sales forecast at _____, a penetration rate of less than a 10th of 1 percent (0.0008) of the estimated 122M women between the ages of 12 and 65 in the U.S. Upon market acceptance and increased demand, we approximate growth rates to grow exponentially and be comparable to other successful new products launched with similar target markets. 2017 Cost Assumptions: _____

2017 Revenue Assumptions:

	2016	2017	2018
Blinger™ Sales (M)			
Refill Pack Sales (M)			
Revenue (M)			
Operating Expenses / Cost of Sales (M)			
Net Profit (M)			

Confidential and Proprietary
GEMC², LLC
ADDRESS
PHONE • EMAIL • WEBSITE

GEMC²'s executive summary.

For me, work and my children are both just magnificent parts of my life. My passion and my loves. I could have my children around me all day, and that would be just perfect. I know not all parents are wired that way, but for me, I love it. Especially now as they're getting older. I want to show them the world, introduce them to different foods, cultures, ideas. I'm raising them with the big picture in mind. I tell them my goal is for them to grow up to be responsible citizens of this country, but that no matter how they turn out as adults, my biggest hope (besides them be-lieving) is that they're kind.

All of us about to enter to give our pitch.

So my personal life crashes right into my business life often, and I'm okay with that. Taking them on a working trip to Maine to audition for *Shark Tank* is just another ordinary day in our lives. A mini adventure on the road of the big one.

When we got to the place where the auditions were held, we waited all day in a winding line in the parking lot to get inside. Once inside, there were chairs set up where we waited to be called. I ran into my friend Shelley Henshaw, creator of Chalk Me Up T-shirts, which are awesome T-shirts, by the way. It was so cool to see her there, and we became even closer friends after that.

Once our turn came, we waited in another line to do our pitch. When we got to the front of that line, we waited for a table to become available. Finally, a woman was free and called us up. She seemed nice, but she was young and maybe a little full of herself. We did our little practiced routine—even the boys had bling in their hair—and gave it our best shot. She looked unimpressed but feigned interest. After our pitch, she tossed my business plan on to a giant pile of other plans in a bin.

I asked her, "Do you have any questions?"

Without looking at us, she barely replied, "Nope. Thank you," then signaled for the person behind us to come forward.

Getting dismissed like that hurt a little. But remember I only had a picture of the plastic model Firm 1 had created for me. I wasn't ready

Even the boys got some bling!

for *Shark Tank*. I knew that. I was glad I did it in any case, because now I get to say, "*Shark Tank* rejected me. Those sillies." (I'm kidding!)

I'm honestly glad, because I learned from the experience, and it helped me understand more about my business. I'm telling you, every failure adds up.

I had heard that failure is a part of success, but I didn't know how true this was till I personally experienced the other side of failure: success. I now have a new perspective. When you're on the journey, it seems to take forever. You don't know—I didn't know—that at some point in the next year, or three, it will have all come to fruition. I'm now in that spot (where you too can be someday, I promise) and able to look back and see how everything added up, the good and the bad, and how most of it actually connected. Failures were a big part of my success. Failure is not a zero on the scorecard of your journey.

Imagine we gave your ultimate goal, the place where you feel you would be successful, a point value of one hundred.

Now let's say all your failures are graded and you earn points with each one (and your wins too—but those are obvious point earners). And there can be negative points with some really big failures, but let's say only up to negative twenty though, as most failures are actually positive, as I hope you'll soon see, or learn for yourself. Most failures will give you points that move you forward toward your hundred-point goal—maybe only two points for this one and three for that one, but if you add those two failures together you're at five points, and you haven't won at all, you've actually failed twice.

Then you get a small win—those happen a lot too, don't forget.

Let's say you got a small investor to come in, and they did a fair equity exchange with you for their cash investment. I'd say that's a twenty-point win. Money is priceless in start-ups.

Then maybe you did something stupid, and there's no way it could be considered a positive failure. Even having learned never to do that again can't give it value. So we'll say it's negative ten points. I really like to see failures as nonevents, rather than as hurtful events (negative points), but in reality, I'm sure there are some failures that will have negative effects on your business. So we'll leave it this way—for this example I'm demonstrating—but for your mindset's sake, try to see them as nonevents or positive small point earners.

So in our scenario, you've had three failures (one big one) and one small win, but when you add up all the numbers (two, three, negative ten, and twenty), you're at fifteen points toward your hundred-point goal. You've moved forward, and you've had more losses than wins.

Do you see? Change your focus that only wins matter. Failures can also add up to wins. This is important for you to get, so you won't feel so devastated when the failures happen. You need to not get down on yourself as much as you can. Focus on the work, not the outcomes. Besides, it's not our setbacks that define us—it's our comebacks. If you keep going, you'll have plenty of those.

Toward the end of my journey, I realized that some of my greatest wins for Blinger, when they happened, started out as, or were total failures. Now, I can see that they were significant advances forward.

One big failure in particular was *key* to my success, but we'll get to that later.

At this point, I had written my business plan and incorporated my business in preparation for *Shark Tank*. Was getting rejected by *Shark Tank* really a setback? Not at all. It was actually more like a four-point failure toward my hundred-point goal. I did a lot of work to put that plan together, a lot of research, and learned a lot about marketing, manufacturing, and financials specific to my product. I was ready to talk to any investor now. Having my business plan was a step forward, not back.

If I had made *Shark Tank* the ultimate goal, then the rejection might have tempted me to think of quitting. But *Shark Tank* wasn't my goal. I didn't need to be on that show and have a Shark be my investor. I knew I would eventually need an investor, or so I thought, to succeed, but there are thousands of investors out there you can pitch. Plus, I didn't really get rejected by the Sharks. It was an admin who worked for the producers of the show. She was not an actual investor. And even if she had been an investor, hers was still just one opinion.

The point is that failures can add up in positive ways. Your knowledge of what to do, and also what you need to stop doing, grows. At a bare minimum, with every failure, you get smarter.

Always remember that no one goes straight up to the top without a lot of detours and dead ends. Not a little. *A lot.* All worthwhile things in life take time. They also require a lot of movement, energy, drive, and understanding that every effort you make isn't always going to work out.

The bottom line is that you cannot succeed without failing. If you're failing, it means you're doing it. It's part of success. I know we've all heard that and you're probably tired of hearing it if you're in the midst of it all, but it's so true. If you're not falling short, hitting roadblocks or even mountains then you're most likely not progressing. Our success is directly tied to our willingness or unwillingness to do what it takes. If you're doing what it takes to achieve your dreams, you should be congratulating yourself right now. And know you have a fan—me. I'm super proud of you! Keep going.

The greatest salespeople, thinkers, and leaders have all dealt with rejection, fear, and tough times. They kept going, kept taking chances, succeeding in the face of failure and despite adversity. You can too.

Failure is known to be such a big part of being successful that I think it's one of the reasons some people don't pursue their dreams. They've heard it so much or they intuitively know it's part of it, and that scares them. I get that. No one likes rejection or to seemingly lose.

But here's the good news, and how my faith operates. Once you identify your biggest fear, you can tell yourself that fear is the enemy. It's a lie from the pits of hell. It's keeping you in your place. Keeping you from your destiny. Keeping you from your God-given purpose, a purpose to make a difference and to have a dream fulfilled. To be a role model to others and maybe by your life be the example of what he can do. And what he does for you is proof he can do it for another. Your job is simply to believe, stay in prayer, and keep moving toward the goal.

We hadn't formally been told no by *Shark Tank*, so there was no reason to think that we *wouldn't* get a call back from them the next week. They told us they would call us by the following Wednesday if we had been chosen. I always hold out the hope, because I just think that things can happen that way. Besides, what good are low hopes?

And while I'm on this, why is it so hard for us to believe we're a beautiful creation of God and so easy to believe something bad about ourselves? The lie. I've always found it much simpler, and nicer, to believe in the good than to believe in the bad. The bad could be false or a rumor; the bad keeps me scared and in my place. The good gives me hope and offers me a brighter future. If he gave us free will, then why choose the bad? Why believe that you're not good enough or it will never happen or you've always failed in the past, so why should this be any different, when you can believe you're amazing, gifted, strong, and smart? And that those failures were only preparing you to come into your greatness with humility and gratefulness in your heart.

I'm genuinely a positive person. Mostly positive, I think. I'm not laughing all day long. I'm serious about a lot. But it's usually positive seriousness. Whatever I was feeling, however, I was pretty sure we hadn't been selected. My kids didn't seem fazed at all. I'm not even sure they knew what was happening. It just didn't feel like a big deal to me or that we'd been rejected. I was still on the same path with the same confidence I had before.

We didn't get the call the following Wednesday, and I really thought my kids wouldn't have even noticed. But they never fail to amaze me. Turns out they were very interested, and even more astounding, it really mattered to them. They had seemed totally bored with the whole pitch thing when we were there and annoyed at how many times I made us practice it. They didn't even talk about it once on the drive home. But the first thing they asked me when I picked them up from school that day was "Did you get the call?"

At first, I was confused, "What call?" I asked.

They all yelled, "From *Shark Tank*! Duh!" looking at me like I was brainless.

"Oh, no, I haven't, but I don't think we will get a call," I told them, still a little confused that they thought we would.

"What!" they yelled simultaneously. "Why do you think that?"

Suddenly I felt like I had a lot of coaching to do or business sales training to teach. They were really upset. In reality, it made sense. This was their first business rejection. And at such young ages. Bless their little hearts.

I wanted to laugh, but I felt bad that they were so upset. I told them, "Guys, this is part of it," and a bunch of other motivational stuff that I can't remember. Although I do remember telling them, "Besides, what a boring story this would make if it was that simple. The best stories are the ones where people overcome these types of challenges and rejections."

I don't know how I knew it was going to be a story then, but I guess I did somehow. And that meant I knew it was going to end up with a good ending too, because most good stories have good endings. I just never lost confidence in my dream—I questioned why I was the one selected to carry it out many times—but the product I always knew would happen.

They were better by Thursday and had totally moved on by the weekend, but it was interesting to see how much they cared. They were paying attention.

I knew there were going to be other seasons of the show, and other times we could try out, if that's what we decided to do. I told them that too—and that when we did, I was sure we'd have the working prototype, so we'd totally make it onto the show.

The night we got back from Maine, I dropped the kids and my mom off at her house. We were going to eat dinner there, but I went over to our house real quick to check on the dogs. When I pulled up, I saw there was a package waiting for me on my steps. I opened it. It was my plastic model, and I loved it.

I quickly drove back to my mom's house and ran inside. I held the model out for everyone to see, I said, "Oh my gosh, look at this!"

It was so exciting to hold. I passed it around to everyone. It was such an amazing moment for me. A 3-D version of my dream. The kids thought it was cool, and even my mom said that it felt like it was "substantial." That was definitely saying something.

First non-working prototype, Firm 1, August 2015.

Chapter 8

"To accomplish great things, we must not only act, but dream; not only plan, but believe."

~**Anatole France**, Nobel Prize–winning author, from a speech at the Académie Française

So now I had a business name and a business plan, but after a terrible battle with Firm 1 and losing nearly half my savings, it was time to find a new engineer. Mind you, at this point it was already September of 2015. Almost a year had passed since I had my dream, and I was starting over with the proposal process. Although this time I was definitely savvier. Here's what I wrote to one of the new engineers I was interviewing, whom I ended up hiring:

Thanks for signing the NDA. I'm sending the design and mechanism concept items for you to see. I'd like to talk to you first, then send CAD files over. This is generally what I've been looking to see in a proposal:

1) Redesign of handle—we need to talk first about this as it's not apparent

2) Confirmation on strip idea or recommendation of other circular design that might work better as far as production or functionality, etc., and then design strip/belt/disc

3) Development of working prototype—one for testing on your end and one for demonstrating on mine

4) Manufacturing files—ready to develop tool and go into production

5) Potential help in connecting me with reputable manufacturers

6) Afterward consulting help with manufacturers and production—will need this since the files will be developed by your company, would need to know that you're available should there be a problem once manufacturing has begun.

That's basically it! :)

Thank you,
Angie

I hired this firm, we'll call them Firm 2, first only for a strip feasibility study for the current design that I really liked, after they thoughtfully addressed all my concerns in their proposal. Here's what they agreed to supply:

- Working rudimentary lab version device with demonstration of applying rhinestones to hair
- Any specifications developed regarding the strip materials and configuration
- Specification for the adhesive used to demonstrate the concept
- Specifications for the rhinestones used to demonstrate

I thought I had made a great decision this time. Firm 2 was American—someone from my own country. (If you live in France, hire someone in France is the point.) Also, Firm 2 was a two-man show—not just one guy running things out of his garage like the last time. They had actual office space!

However, after I hired them, they sent along a concept of a more linear design, one my contact explained would need fewer total parts and meet the target cost of five to seven dollars. But I wasn't interested in a new design—especially not the one he supplied, which, in my opinion, looked like a see-through stapler. I had fallen in love with the plastic model Firm 1 had created. I thought it was cute, like an ice cream cone. Cute shape. Cute colors. It was frustrating to me that this new design looked nothing like that.

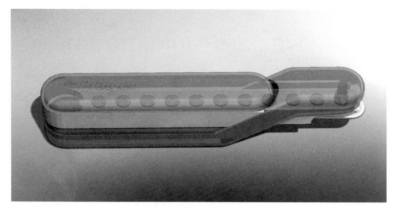

Stapler concept design.

Firm 2 shared that they had concerns with the circular strip model, but still, this new concept design didn't look like it was going to work much better to me. Used the way they proposed, it would have the plastic strip sticking out of the top and getting in the way when you put the next rhinestone in your hair. It was tricky sometimes working with men who don't do anything with their hair. They naturally don't understand why having a flexible piece of plastic jutting out of the device, with possible leftover adhesive residue on it, would make it cumbersome and challenging to use.

Therefore, in order to use this design, you'd have to tear off the strip after each stone, or every other one, was placed. Then, if the strip was perforated to make this tearing easier, you'd still run the risk of having it tear when you took it out of the package—before you even got it into the device—or tear in the device as it advanced. It may have been less costly to make and less complicated to load, but I didn't like it and didn't think other women would either.

I was also frustrated that he hadn't done what I asked. He didn't supply a study on our current design. I found that communication was the issue many times when working with engineers. I believe it's hard to work with people of the opposite gender sometimes and especially those who are in fields you don't have much knowledge about.

TOP FIVE COMMUNICATION TIPS

Here are some tips I picked up as a woman working with male engineers.

1 **Use collective pronouns.** This protects you because it makes it less about you (I, me), and more about the company (we, us). It doesn't hurt to create the idea that you have a staff that might include some big scary dude who could pop out at any time if anyone messes with you.

2 **Don't share too much.** Be careful how much you divulge about your personal life. Being an open book and a single woman doing this on my own and oversharing, my natural way, hurt me a few times. Some people will try to take advantage of you if they can. Protect yourself. You can still be kind and friendly and stay who you are. Just be careful about what you share with anyone you do business with and especially your private business challenges, particularly if you're a woman.

3 **Take it slow.** Give yourself time to think before you respond. This was one of my biggest downfalls. I didn't always read emails or texts carefully or slowly and reacted many times when I should have taken a step back to think things through. Sometimes it was inevitable. As a single mom working from home, I rushed through most things before I got pulled away by the next thing, like my kids, but there were many times I wish I had taken more time to get a clearer perspective before replying. Taking that extra day could have saved me a couple of years of work—and I'm not exaggerating when I say this.

4 **Don't ever respond when you're mad.** You can write the email, but don't send it. Take a day to think about it. Share it with a trusted, levelheaded person first, at least. For me, that person ended up becoming my daughter Cambria. As she grew on this journey, she became more and more a

person I could turn to for composed, sensible advice. For me, my emotions are my center, which can be a detriment. For her, she's more even-keeled and cool-headed. She has always helped to see another side, or how I might respond differently—even when she was as young as eleven. I have enormous admiration for her for that. (And simmer down, you other kids. You'll get your shoutout.) Glenn, my attorney, has also been this person for me many times. Oh, and of course my business partner, the big man himself. Find that person in your life who centers you, who helps you see the world from different eyes, and bring that person in when you need to get a better perspective before you send that email.

5 **Try to understand first before being understood.** You hired this person or company for a reason—remind them and yourself of this. Ask questions. Some people may not have had as strong of a personality as me but were brilliant at what they did. There were times I needed to give them encouragement to basically just speak up. To let them know they didn't have to be afraid of me and that I wanted their input, even if it seemed like it would be against what I was thinking was best. I had to be quiet and patient as they put their words together, which is extremely hard for me to do, but also extremely important. I know this may sound funny, but when I know I need to be quiet and just listen, I sit on my hands. I don't know why, but it works. You can try this out on your next call if you're like me.

When I wrote to Firm 2, I told them that we didn't like the new design, that it wasn't nearly as cute or appealing as our current model, and we wanted to determine the validity of *that* concept. Just because we wanted it to work more like a tool didn't mean we wanted it to look like a tool. I basically reiterated that we still wanted the feasibility study done on the other model, our first concept Firm 1 had come up with.

Firm 2 didn't push back on me when I wrote this to them, nor did they remind me of something they'd already shared with me—"that the design as it stood had significant plastic part design challenges and was going to need to be changed in order for it to function as intended." I saw that line in an email from five years ago when writing this book. It stands out like a sore thumb now, but I can bet at the moment I didn't take the time to properly process it—that I probably read it in the school pickup line with two kids singing or arguing over chips in the back seat of the car. And instead of Firm 2 standing behind what they had written and for what they knew to be true, they just went along with what I wanted.

The problem with non-engineers, like me, leading the show is that things can naturally turn out wrong. I didn't understand all the nuances of how engineering worked, and the guy I hired, who knew better, didn't reiterate his concerns or speak up about what he knew could lead to future issues—either with the device functionality itself or for product costs for my business. This was going to create some problems later. Good communication—especially tip five, if you're a strong, driven type, which I think most entrepreneurs are—will help you. It's so vital to your success in these situations. Both sides need to listen with the aim of understanding and achieving the end goal. But this was my product in the end, so it was on me to make sure the communication was clear, not the people I hired. You are the one who owns all of it, the good and the bad, you can't blame others for mistakes or misunderstandings. This is on you to win or lose, the onus is yours.

At the time I hired Firm 2, I could only afford the first three milestones, which didn't include a functioning prototype. That was milestone four. I was going to need more funds, so I borrowed $15,000 from my mom.

I knew I was going to need more money than that to take my device to market, but I believed that once I had a working prototype, I could find investors. So on my direction, Firm 2 took the plastic model design Firm 1 had come up with and started working on turning it into an actual functioning prototype. Cuteness won over practicality.

It was around this time that I learned about crowdfunding, and in fact, one of the best things I did to build my business was to run a Kickstarter campaign. But probably not for the reasons you might think.

Kickstarter is a funding platform for creative projects. Basically, you ask people to support your project, or, in my case, to *buy* my product, before it's even been made. This allows funds to come into your business, which you can use to produce whatever it is you're making without giving up equity in your company. In exchange, you provide the product at a reduced amount—or they get to be the first to ever have the product or a special experience. The rewards they receive for backing your idea are customized by you, based on what seems fair to the dollar amount they give.

I learned about Kickstarter after watching an interesting documentary called *FrackNation* by journalist Phelim McAleer. This note ran before the end credits:

"*FrackNation* was funded by 3,305 backers on Kickstarter who generously donated $212,265 to have us investigate the truth about fracking. All funds from oil and gas companies or their executives were explicitly rejected. *FrackNation* is a film by the people, for the people."

I was blown away. Other people had funded McAleer's dream? Strangers all over the world. I thought that Blinger could be funded by other people too. That really got me excited about getting the funds necessary and without losing half my company to an investor that might have a different mission than mine. It made me even more relieved that I hadn't been given the opportunity to make a deal with a Shark, who would have taken a significant share of my company in exchange for an investment.

I didn't fully understand at the time how Kickstarter really worked though. In my thinking, if I had a great product, which God and I knew we did, I could sell it via Kickstarter and raise enough capital necessary to build the tool and manufacture it.

This was all nice in theory, but what I learned from doing one, two, and then ultimately three Kickstarters is that you need so much more than a good idea and a good product to be successful with crowdfunding.

I looked into hiring a video production company to film my Kickstarter, but the cost ranged anywhere from $5,000 to $10,000. Luckily, there's an amazing art school in our area, Cab Calloway School of the Arts, and so one of my friends suggested that I ask the Communication Arts Department if they would lend us a couple of their seniors to film my Kickstarter as an extra-credit assignment, and use the school's professional video equipment as well. Great idea!

I asked the head of that department, and he said "Yes." So in the end, all of our video was filmed for free.

I wrote the script and got everything else in place while Firm 2 was getting the prototype engineered. It was all coming together.

In early January, Firm 2 finished and mailed me my first working prototype! It was so exciting. He sent seventeen strips as well that we filled with rhinestones and Swarovski crystals. We were ready to film our Kickstarter!

First working prototype and strips, Firm 2, January 2016.

Unfortunately, the prototype was eighteen plastic parts and was almost twice as big as Firm 1's plastic model. It didn't turn out as *cute* as I hoped, but it worked, and I was thrilled. I knew we were on our way.

I knew the prototype had to have as few parts as possible—ideally, fewer than ten. I recently read that in the business plan I had written before I even hired Firm 2. There it was, in black and white. So why didn't I press for this in the early days of actually making the prototype for Blinger? Because it got lost in the million other details I was trying to juggle or figure out. I also pushed for this design, if you remember, and the engineers didn't push back. I trusted them too much and didn't have good advisers with experience in this field working with me. So the engineers, in their defense, were building the device I wanted. By the time we got to prototype, it was kind of too late.

I also believed they wouldn't have designed something that didn't make sense for the manufacturing or marketing of it. I know better now. You have to stand up again and again and again for what you know is best for your business. The engineer is not going to be there when you're attempting to convince a retailer to put your eighty-dollar Blinger (that should be twenty dollars) on their shelves. You own the whole process, beginning to end. The numbers do have to work in the end or it won't work. I went from too much involvement about my business from Firm 1 to not enough from Firm 2.

In my (and possibly Firm 2's) defense, we saw this as a hair tool, not a toy. I've paid over $100 for a flat iron. Still, for this product, eighteen plastic parts was about eight too many.

Thankfully, the future is not ours to see. At that moment, I knew I was on my way. I had a "film crew," I had a prototype, I had a couple of girls from my kids' school to participate as models—as well as my own kids. I was all set. We filmed our first Kickstarter video on Saturday, January 9, 2016.

After filming, we sent the prototype back to Firm 2 to continue development and resolve some functioning issues.

While they handled that, I worked on images, logo design, packaging concepts, and getting our Kickstarter pages and website set up and ready to go live. Here is our first logo.

Then we dropped the "The." Always drop the "The." Here is our second logo.

A few months later, we finally launched our Kickstarter. We set a goal of $150,000, because that was legitimately the minimum we determined we needed to get through the tooling and manufacturing of ten thousand devices. What I didn't know then but I would soon learn was that in order to have a successful Kickstarter, you needed to spend $50,000 to $75,000 in marketing before you launch—or have a huge supportive network you can tap.

Plus, crowdfunding brings with it a crowd mentality. With Kickstarter, if your supporters don't think you can hit your money goal or see it happening quickly, then they won't back it. But if it starts doing well, people will back it just to be a part of it.

It became clear immediately that we weren't going to hit the $150,000 mark, and that we should have started with a lower goal then hopefully grown it to the actual amount we needed. Another thing that is important to understand about a crowd fund is that if you don't hit your funding goal, you don't get any of the funds. So if we raised $149,000, we wouldn't get any of it. You have to raise all the funds to get the money. And, unfortunately, the only way to change the dollar goal is to launch a new Kickstarter, so that's what we did. We took down our first Kickstarter, and a week later we relaunched a new one with a $50,000 goal, which we again quickly learned was still too high.

While Kickstarter one and then two were happening, I was also having some personal issues having to do with the custody of my children. I won't get into the details here, but this dispute was taxing, time-consuming, and draining on all of us. I was distracted from Arbonne and Blinger many times to fight these battles for the benefit of my children. The rest of my life wasn't stopping so I could focus on my businesses.

It's important to realize and accept that while you're working toward your dream, all kinds of things could get in your way—not just business setbacks, but personal things too. Despite what's happening around you, you still need to find a way to move forward. Life is hard sometimes, and boy, can we get derailed. But don't let that stop you. Take a break, focus on other priorities in your life, and then get back on your path toward your goals. You can do it.

There are some mental tricks that I used too, that you can do to help you get through tough spots and keep your dream alive or even to kick off your dream. For one, you can apply what my mom always said to me when I faced tough decisions. Ask yourself, "What's the worst that can happen?" Once you've identified what the worst-case scenario is, unless you're dying, I think you'll find it's usually not that bad.

Another technique that works for me is to first identify what it is that's preventing me from doing this thing that could benefit me or my family. A lot of times, I find it's either pride or some fear (which in Arbonne we used to say is False Evidence Appearing Real). If I realize it's pride, though I ask myself:

What would God think if I did this? If God is okay with something, then why am I letting my neighbor's opinion stop me? Do they really have that much power over my life? Or, an even better question, why am I giving them that much power over my life?

I love Pastor Joel Osteen and listen to him all the time. His messages guided me throughout my journey. He's an amazing speaker, writer, and pastor. He does so much to encourage others to live their best life, to forgive and to love one another, to know and follow Jesus, and even how to handle the ups and downs of everyday life in our fallen world. He's not known for humor necessarily, but he likes to tell a joke before his sermons. He once shared a joke that I think is not only funny, but so true: "In your twenties, you wonder what everyone thinks of you. Then in your forties, you don't care what anyone thinks of you. Then in your sixties, you realize no one was ever thinking of you."

The point is, your neighbor doesn't really care what you do. Your neighbor has their own things to deal with. Unless you run around naked in your neighborhood, no one is wondering about you. Of course, when you get started, there will be a little talk about the delusional choice you're making, but don't worry, eventually everyone will move on back to their own life decisions.

Now, if I realize my block stems from some fear or worry, I acknowledge that fear is a tool the enemy wields, and I tell myself to grow a pair—in the name of Jesus, of course. I know that fear is a lie and, thanks to my faith, I know that I'm safe. "What the enemy will try to use against me, God will use *for* me" (Genesis 50:20). And as for worry, it explicitly says throughout the Bible that we are not to waste one second of our life on worry. "Can all your worries add a single moment to your life?" (Matthew 6:27).

Fear is a prison and to worry is to be its slave.

The best thing you can do to overcome your own self-sabotage, or really, to get over anything, is to identify the block. Once you do, you'll be able to use these formulas any time you're thinking of *not* pursuing something. I pray you'll find yourself set free. Don't worry about your neighbor or friend or the mom behind you in the school pickup line. She won't think you're crazy when you're in your dream car. She's going to be your bestie and want to come over to your new dream home with all her kids! You might even set her free too. Maybe she'll start sharing her own set of crazy ideas with you. You could be her inspiration.

In any case, I'm sure there are companies that launched on Kickstarter that were able to take their product all the way, fulfill all their orders, and also have enough product and capital left over to take it to market by their Kickstarter campaign alone, but I do think they're rare. This never happened for me (and I ended up doing three of them). I'm not knocking Kickstarter or crowdfunding. I'm just saying that it most likely will not work as a replacement to bringing on an investor. However, I highly recommend crowdfunding campaigns (there's more than just Kickstarter, there's also Indiegogo, Crowd Supply, CrowdFunder, and many others), as there are many unexpected benefits you can gain from doing one. Even failed campaigns can open up doors of opportunity.

Remember how I said failure is part of success? I hope so, I only talked about it for a whole chapter! Well, my second Kickstarter was that *key failure* I mentioned. It turned out to be instrumental in making Blinger what it is today. In fact, because of where it led me, two and a half years later, I could link Blinger's success all the way back to that loss. Though my expectations of my Kickstarter and what I really got from it didn't match, it turned out, in the end, it didn't matter.

CROWDFUNDING CHECKLIST

I used Kickstarter, but these tips can probably apply to any crowdsourcing site you use.

- **Set a funding goal.** You want to get the most out of your campaign, but if you shoot too high, you're going to lose it all. For that reason, you need to come up with a minimum funding goal. When you work out the numbers, be sure you're considering: the cost of completion; cost of fulfillment; any legal fees; costs of PR and marketing (see below); platform and processing fees (at the time of this writing, Kickstarter takes 5 percent for platform fees and between 3 and 5 percent for payment processing fees). Also note, the funds you raise are taxable.

- **Secure your first 30 percent.** Before launching your campaign, reach out to friends and family and ask them to pledge ahead of time. You want to get 30 percent of your funding goal before you launch. Then, on day one of your launch, everyone who agreed to back you should go in and make their pledge. This will create a big momentum for your campaign and cause the metrics to boost your page on the crowdfunding site, which gets other people you don't know to notice and hopefully back you. It's a great tip that I wish I had known. I probably would have taken it a step further and collected credit card and shipping info, then placed all the orders myself. People are busy—if you get a yes from someone and you've already got them on the phone, get the money then. They may forget the day of the launch, or you may not ever get them on the phone again. Don't cause double work for you or them.

- **Quality counts.** Spend time on how you tell your story and really invest in how well you tell it, with professional writing, graphics, and a video—which needs to be factored into your PR and marketing costs. The care you put into your video and site will be reflected in how much people care to support you. Sure, you can put out an amateur video, but that will make you look like an amateur—and why would someone want to back you if you don't look serious or capable? Kickstarter makes it sound like any old video shot on your iPhone will work. I'm not sure I believe that to be the case.

- **Get outside interest before you get started.** You'll want as many people as possible to know about your campaign before you launch. Something I wish I'd done before ours was to create a prelaunch page to help get people to subscribe to our email list. This creates an audience much bigger and stronger than the people you already have in your contacts list. It also brings your message to people who are actively interested in supporting crowdfunding campaigns—not just people who will back you because they love you.

- **Alert the media.** This includes the big-time media outlets and journalists but also bloggers. Make sure you have a professional press release ready. Be open to doing interviews with bloggers especially, as many will have a wide audience of followers interested in exactly what you're offering.

- **Grow your social media presence.** You can build followers and interest in your product way before you launch and shoot out regular updates once you do. Again, this helps you reach out to people beyond family and friends. Twitter, Facebook and Instagram all have different etiquettes for when and what to post. Don't post the same thing on all three. Look into best practices and follow them.

Chapter 9

"You are not defined by your past. You are prepared by your past."

~*Joel Osteen*, American televangelist, theologian, speaker, and author

Sometimes things don't work out so that there's room for other things that will. My first two Kickstarters weren't successful, but God knew it wasn't the time or the way things were supposed to work out. While I didn't succeed in achieving the funding goal with my first two Kickstarters, doing them opened many doors for me, with opportunities I would not have had if I hadn't put myself out there.

The first of these unexpected opportunities came to me a couple days after launching my second Kickstarter. I got a voice mail from a guy who worked for an As Seen on TV (ASTV) company, saying, "You don't have to spend any more money. We're gonna take care of everything from manufacturing to marketing. We're gonna do all the work and fund everything, and you can just sit back and collect checks."

When I called him back, after googling them and determining they weren't a scam, we hit it off right away. He explained that they had found me through my Kickstarter. He reiterated that the licensing would be of no cost to me—that they'd make the tool in China, manufacture the product, handle all the aspects of development from then on, and do a national TV campaign. I would still own the product, but they would take over all capital and development risks for the term of the contract. I was going to make about thirty-five cents a Blinger. It didn't seem like much, but I wondered if it could be if it took off.

My main contact suggested I call one of their inventors as a reference. I called Michael Berardi, inventor of the XHose and many other inventions. He had brought them many ideas over the years, and he was the nicest guy. He said to me, "Angie, at some point, if the idea takes off, it's more than enough money. Plus, they do all the work. I don't want to take on all those overhead costs and all that risk if I don't have to."

ASTV reaching out to me at that time made me think maybe this had been God's plan all along. He knew I was struggling through a horrible custody battle. My time and my resources were limited. Maybe he wanted to give me a backup income to my Arbonne business, so that I'd be able to focus on my children full-time. I figured that this was it. God was making sure we were good. With that in my mind, that someone wanted to license my product and take over all the work and lay out all this expense was destiny to me. It wasn't hard to convince me to say yes.

LICENSING AGREEMENT TIPS

Here are some things to push for in your license agreement. Every deal is different, and every licensee works differently, but it's good to know what's possible.

- **Ownership of patents and trademarks.** Basically, you want to retain all rights to the IP. You'll also want to own any improvements they may make to the product. I know many inventors who assign it all to the company and simply collect a lump sum instead of earning royalties throughout the life of the product. It's really about what makes the most sense for you. The royalty license has more risk but also the potential for greater reward.

- **Quality control.** Be sure to have some approval mechanisms in place so that the licensee can't launch an inferior product and hurt your company name.
- **Minimum marketing spend.** Be sure your agreement includes the amount the licensee agrees to spend each year marketing your product. It could be a minimum fixed amount or a percentage of annual sales.
- **Minimum guarantees or minimum annual payments.** This is the minimum amount paid to you each year, regardless of actual sales, and is typically included in an exclusive license. If your licensee doesn't meet the minimum payment, the rights revert back to you, or the agreement gets converted to a nonexclusive license.
- **Initial payment.** This will vary depending on how ready for market your product is. It can also be negotiated in relation to the royalty rate offered—for example, you may have a high initial payment with a lower royalty, or vice versa. In some cases, the initial payment can be counted as an advance against royalties. While this is acceptable, it should be made clear that the initial payment is nonrefundable (they won't get the money back if they don't sell anything).
- **Royalty rate.** The royalty percentage depends on the type of product you're selling, as well as your own experience and track record, with rates typically varying from 3 to 5 percent.
- **Net sales.** The royalty rate will typically be a percentage of net sales, which is the total gross sales minus identified deductible expenses of the licensee. The deductible expenses should be kept to a minimum, and in cases where flexibility is needed, consider putting a cap on the percentage the licensee is allowed to deduct when calculating net sales.
- **Milestones.** The licensee must meet certain milestones by certain dates, with a defined penalty written into the contract for missing these dates.

- **Minimum number of samples.** I would request at least six samples for each stock-keeping unit (sku) made.
- **Brand extension.** Ensure they can't launch other products using any of your patented product items or trademarks without also paying you a royalty on those new items. You should be compensated the same royalty for brand extensions, because your IP and your brand are what get the new product on the shelves in the first place. Without your product, those line extensions wouldn't exist.
- **Terms.** These range anywhere from one to five years, and there can be auto-renewals built in.
- **Indemnification.** You indemnify the licensee, which means you will cover their expenses, fees, damages, etc. should someone sue them alleging the licensed product infringes on their patent or trademark. Many licensees will try to convince you it's standard. I would recommend highly that you fight for your agreement not to indemnify the licensee or at a minimum only indemnify them up to a certain percentage of your royalty earnings, like 10 to 30 percent.
- **Option to buy.** This includes allowing you to buy all unsold product, including tools, at cost, if the license isn't renewed for any reason.

After we worked out the agreement, ASTV basically took over everything but kept me involved—as much or as little as I wanted to be, which I appreciated. My main contact and I had a blast working together and I was thankful to be able to learn so much about the manufacturing process. Plus, picking out the colors for the device, getting a new and better logo designed, and being able to help with the stone selections was much more enjoyable to me than all the technical stuff I'd been dealing with.

This particular ASTV group was also in the same state as Swarovski's corporate office. Swarovski crystals are precision-cut glass that sparkle like diamonds. My contact at ASTV knew my passion for Swarovski crystals, and when he let me know we'd be launching with their crystals, I almost fainted. The way the light catches them is truly dazzling, like a diamond, and so they're just stunning in the hair.

After ASTV stepped in, Firm 2 started getting a little short with me. I sensed at the time they wanted to stay involved through the manufacturing process because they could earn more money; I later learned this was exactly the case. It was understandable; they were a business. But at this point, I only needed Firm 2 to finish up the final milestone I'd hired them for, the manufacturing drawings, which I then turned over to ASTV's manufacturing partner in China. That seemed like the end of the journey for Firm 2 and Blinger.

That summer, I met my contact from ASTV at the home of the woman who was going to produce our commercial. She was famous in the infomercial space, so I was excited when she agreed to do our Blinger commercial.

I liked her immediately. She was sharp, classy, and had a cool air about her. I had told ASTV that I wanted to share a verse or just something about my faith in the commercial, to give God the glory, and it seemed like they had alerted her of this (sometimes it feels like being a believer is similar to having a disease everyone's warned about before you get there). Shortly after I arrived, she gently pulled me aside and explained how the TV channels she worked with wouldn't allow any mention of God or anything religious-sounding to air on their stations. I told her I understood but that it was a shame.

I didn't necessarily expect anyone to let me share my faith, but I always asked. "If you don't ask, how can you receive?" (Matthew 7: 7–8). I just didn't want to not give credit where credit was due. I did my part, but the dream, and many occurrences to come, were from God. He set it all up, and I stumbled through it, doing my best to trust and honor what he wanted done.

Later that day, everyone was talking about how a rapper had joked on TV about how he'd roofied a girl and gotten away with it. The producer said she'd never watch that station again, to which I boldly said, "Yeah, but let's not talk about God on TV."

It wasn't a jab at her, and I could tell she knew that. It was a jab at the crazy restrictions there are about sharing faith, and our even more insane (to me, anyway) looseness about sharing immoral things all the time and everywhere.

Everyone got quiet after that, and I'll never forget the look on her face. I believe it resonated with her. I hope so. The ones with power need to make their voices heard.

These things remind me of what Miss Clara said in the movie *War Room*, "Everyone's always trying to leave Jesus out, which is one reason we're in the mess we're in."

Though I killed the energy in the room, I was happy. I felt like I stood up for God. I was proud of myself. Or, as Kathie Lee Gifford says in her household, "Groud" (she puts the God in proud). It was one of those moments in life when you think of the perfect thing to say at the perfect moment it should be said—not five hours later while you're cooking dinner.

One other thing that came out of that meeting was that we decided to change the name from Blinger to Hair Blinger, the thinking being that people would understand the product quicker.

New product name, Hair Blinger, and third logo.

As we headed out to lunch, I called Go Daddy and bought www. hairblinger.com. Over lunch, my ASTV friend said, "I've got to see if we can get the Hair Blinger domain name."

"Oh, I already bought it on the way here," I told him.

"Okay, that's awesome!" he said, though sounding a little shocked.

Like I've said, I don't spend much time thinking about doing things—I just do them. Sometimes it works out.

A couple of months after signing with ASTV, I got an email from ABC, which had also found me from my Kickstarter. Just another good thing to come out of my crowdfunding *failure*. They wanted to interview me for a new show with Steve Harvey. A reality TV show that gave entrepreneurs the chance to win money for their business. I adore Steve Harvey, and the kids and I were so excited. We were jumping around the living room, me holding my laptop trying to finish reading the email while we all freaked out. I saw this as a huge opportunity for us, and I couldn't believe we were being considered for national television because of Blinger—excuse me, Hair Blinger. It was amazing!

The casting agent asked me to submit a video with my product to introduce myself, demonstrate how it works, and share what makes it unique, then discuss how much money I needed and what that money would be used for.

I'm not a fan of the camera, and putting makeup on is challenging for me. I'm so not a girly-girl. (I know it's weird—I mean, my whole livelihood is selling skincare and makeup products to women with Arbonne, and now I was trying to sell a shiny blingy thingy to women everywhere.) But I embraced it as best as I could, and Cambria and I began filming.

We had to submit take after take of different videos that summer. It was grueling work. We had lines to memorize, furniture to move, lighting and cameras to set up, then lighting and cameras to figure out. Not to mention having our hair, makeup, and clothes just right each time—

plus getting a twelve-year-old to participate during her summer break, plus two boys and a two-year-old to sit still and be quiet—good times!

Once we were accepted as contestants, they sent this ginormous contract. It basically said they could use any footage they filmed, from any point in the process, wherever, however, and as much as they wanted, anytime and anywhere they wanted. I remember reading that in bed with all my kids lying there next to me. (They all had their own beds; they just liked to sleep in mine, at least until we all started not to fit.) I said out loud to all of them, "Well, I guess we're not going on TV. I'm not signing this thing."

Cambria bolted up. "What!"

I was mostly kidding, but I was also genuinely concerned. I know me and I know sometimes—scratch that, I know *often*—I say things without really thinking them through. And having that precise combination of orneriness and bravery in my DNA, these things I'd say were sometimes a little too scrappy for the public to hear.

I told her, "You know I'm going to say something stupid-sounding or outrageous and then they're going to have it out there forever. Do you want that? And if you think I embarrass you now, wait till something I say goes viral and people play it on a loop for the rest of your life."

I was truly concerned. I basically just call it out when I see things. It's not like it's *always* a bad thing, and people usually *kind of* like this about me. But for my teenage daughter, it can be a little horrifying.

Of course I signed the contract. And then I prayed big prayers.

At first I was going for $50,000. Then they asked if I'd go on for $25,000, which meant another set of videos on what I'd do with that amount. They knew I had a licensing deal, so they didn't see a real need for me to win much money, but they liked me and wanted to find a way to get me on. And I wanted the publicity for my product. Then a few days later they asked if I'd go on for $10,000. At that point

I said, "Look, to be on national television with Steve Harvey? I would *pay you* $10,000."

The crux of the show was that two entrepreneurs would go head-to-head demonstrating their product. Then the audience would vote on who they thought should get the money. But before they announced the winner, Steve would have the contestants come to the middle of the stage and give them a chance at a cash-out option. If you thought you weren't going to win, you could hit this big button and win a lower dollar amount. If you were wrong, then that's all you got. You wouldn't get the higher amount even if you won. If you were right, then both entrepreneurs left winners—you with a small amount and the other with the targeted bigger amount.

I knew this was going to be an amazing, life-changing experience. I mean, it was Steve Harvey, how could it not be? I already had two of his books: *Act Like a Lady, Think Like a Man,* which was about romance and which I'd already read, and *Act Like a Success, Think Like a Success,* which was about business and which I quickly started reading that weekend. The one on business has really helped me. If I ever got out of the house, maybe the one on romance would too.

I also knew I needed to work out a situation with ASTV that when the show aired, I'd get paid in full on those sales from the TV show. Part of my agreement stated that anything I sold, outside of them, I would get paid full price, minus the cost to make it.

I wanted to make sure that on the website they were developing, there would be a way to indicate how the sale came in, maybe a drop-down menu asking, "How did you hear about Hair Blinger?" I wanted them to list Steve Harvey's show name, which I would soon find out was going to be called *Steve Harvey's Funderdome.* But there was some pushback on this from ASTV, and this bothered me.

I ended up talking to the owner, who told me, "Angie, you know everybody thinks it's going to be this big thing when you're on

TV, but you're probably really not going to get a lot of sales from the show."

At the time, I thought he was saying this because he didn't want to pay me more. I mean, this was national television. ABC. Steve Harvey. A new show—not just a commercial. On top of that, it would be me, this amazing saleslady, single mom of four, representing this darling woman's product. Who wasn't going to love that and want to support the kids and me by buying a Hair Blinger? I was sure he was wrong.

I had our filming date confirmed by ABC, and it was around the same time the production units were going to be in from China. The timing seemed perfect. I thought I would have an actual manufactured, retail-ready device, and not Firm 2's diminishing prototype, to film with. But all of a sudden, a few weeks after the website discussion, ASTV stopped getting back to me.

I wrote an email to the owner, and my lawyer, Glenn, sent a formal letter. They finally responded, and they overnighted the production piece to me.

I was so excited to get it, only to quickly realize why they had been avoiding me: it didn't work.

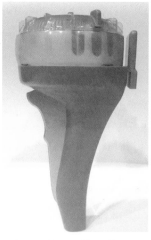

First production Hair Blinger,
ASTV, October 2016.

Our new logo—loved it!

The white drum part that rotates with the strip inside was made out of a material called Delrin, which needs to cool in a controlled manner (unlike other materials, like ABS plastic, which is what most of the device is made of) after it's been molded or it will contract to below specifications. In other words, if Delrin-molded pieces are not cooled properly, they will shrink. The interior part, the drum, was made of Delrin, not ABS, and was clearly not cooled properly. It was smaller than the length of the strips. Because of this, the strips didn't fit inside and would pop up. This caused the stones to misalign, so they couldn't be pushed out without jamming inside the device.

DRUM

White Delrin drum inside device.

I would learn all these hows and whys later. The bottom line was that my production Hair Blinger was useless. I'd have to film with my 3-D-printed paper prototype, which was on its last legs.

If that wasn't bad enough, I also learned that even though the product they made wasn't working, they were still going to go ahead with a commercial and send out faulty Hair Blingers. They wanted to test the market before Christmas, and if it was positive, then they would fix the issues. But in the meantime, they'd be ticking off about three hundred people.

That was not acceptable to me. It was still my product. It was my company name that would be affected. It could have ruined my reputation in the marketplace—especially nowadays with online reviews.

"You can't do that," I told them. I had quality controls written into the contract, thankfully, and they knew it.

This all happened a few days before I was to leave for Los Angeles to film with Steve Harvey. Glenn wrote a termination letter, and in the end the split was actually amicable. The owner didn't put up much of a fight and handled it with grace. He signed the letter and sent it right back.

Also happening during this time: I won my custody battle, and I finally had the arrangement that made the most sense for my children.

In a sense, I had given away my Hair Blinger dream to ASTV, and now it was all back. It was truly amazing how God meant it to stay with me (this wouldn't be the first time I would give it away, only to get it back). In this instance, he knew I just needed some breathing space to deal with the issues in my personal life, and he created a way for that to happen.

Chapter 10

"Trials teach us what we are; they dig up the soil and let us see what we are made of."

~**Charles Spurgeon**, preacher and one of Christianity's most prolific writers

In October of 2016, I headed to LA to compete on *Funderdome*. I took Cambria with me, to be my model, while my mom watched Grace and my boys back at home.

Hollywood has strict laws on taking care of kids in the TV and movie business, making sure they're getting a good education, and although Cambria had only this one gig, she had tutors on set the entire time we were in Los Angeles. Even when it wasn't a school day, if she was on the set, she had her tutor there with her. And on school days, when we weren't on the set, her tutor was with us at the hotel. Her own personal companion was always with her.

When we arrived, we found out they had to move our filming date back about four days, so we ended up staying a full week in LA. It was awesome! We had a lovely hotel room with a full kitchen. It was a beautiful week for us that I'll never forget and a great experience for her. I loved that I was able to bring her with me.

I don't like being on camera. I know you know. And there was good reason. The camera doesn't like me either. This isn't a joke or just in my mind. I have proof. The first day I was on the ABC set, I walked up to my wardrobe rack, which was identified by my picture attached to it. The guy looked at the picture, then at me, then back to the picture, then back at me. I made a comment about how I'm not very photogenic, and he said, "Oh yeah, you look nothing like your picture." As if he was disgusted by the photo.

I wasn't insulted. I was thankful that another person also didn't think that I looked as bad in real life as I did in my photos. In all sincerity, I replied, "Oh, thank you so much. You just made my day."

I'm also not great at following a script. I had to memorize only one page, and it was in like size-fourteen font, but I couldn't memorize it to save my life. Not the ideal TV participant. Maybe this is why I went east instead of west in my twenties! I don't know if it's something with my age or my brain or my nerves, but Cambria would stop me with, "No, Mom, you're supposed to say this," and I just could not get it right, even though I practiced constantly. I took that piece of paper everywhere with me. We'd be walking around LA and I'd be practicing that dang script. My one-page script.

On top of that, I was stressing out because the prototype was starting to fall apart, and I spent the week running around town trying to buy stuff to stop the pieces from breaking off. In testing with it, I wouldn't be able to get one gem to come out till the fifth punch or so. Then, other times, the first one would come out, followed by three or four more before it would fail again. There was no consistency. It was becoming more and more nerve-racking the closer we got to filming.

The day of the shoot, we had a call time really early in the morning. I had a room with my name on the door—which I just thought was so cool, so celebrity-like. All my production pieces were already onstage, so the stylist had to manually put the crystals in my hair with glue dots, which are not safe for your hair.

While I was in the chair getting made up, two *Dancing with the Stars* hairstylists came over. They were in a different studio but had heard about Hair Blinger and had come to see my product. They were asking me all these questions—and saying how much they wanted and needed one. They even started helping to put a lot of the stones in my hair. I was so nervous about the show, I never got their contact information, but I wish I had that conversation on film. It was the coolest thing, how much they were into my product and wanting it to style performers for their show. I was so happy Cambria was there to hear it. She was always supportive, but she was also a child. I wondered sometimes if she thought I was nuts for pursuing this hair-bling thing. I may not care much for what others think of me, but I *do care* what my children think of me.

When it was our turn, Cambria and I headed to the set. I was ready to vomit. I'm not afraid of talking to people, as I did that for a living. I wasn't even afraid to talk in front of an audience. I did that every month at our Arbonne meetings.

You know what it was. Yep, just the stupid cameras weirding me out.

They announced my name, and that was my cue to run (I mean *onstage*). I did my best to seem confident. My opening seemed pretty good, a little fake-sounding—one of the main reasons I hate scripts—but I was feeling it could have been worse. I then invited Cambria out so I could bling her hair. She looked adorable—wearing a dress, which is a rarity for her (she's my cowgirl).

Cambria and I on the set of Funderdome. *That is one stressed-out smile I'm wearing.*

We came to the moment of truth—time to demonstrate the product. I separated out a section of her hair and slid it into the slot on the Hair Blinger. I held my breath, and I know she was holding hers. Ready to do the first punch, I pulled the handle and prayed. We wouldn't know if the gem was placed until I moved the device down to punch out the next one. As I moved it, I saw it had. I know there was a sigh of relief in my voice. I still had to talk while doing all this. Then I moved down and punched the second one. Moving again, I saw the second gem was in her hair. I was starting to feel elated.

Then I punched the third, and as I moved the device down, I saw it hadn't left a gem. I still went ahead and punched the fourth one—it's all the same motion—but I knew it wouldn't be there either. Once the device was jammed, it was done. It killed my confidence that only two came out. The audience saw all of it too; the cameraman had zoomed in on me and we were on full display on the screen behind us.

Blinger's moment of truth played in promotion trailers for the show!
I still hold my breath when I see this image.

My voice cracked on every other word from then on. I kept trying to relax and be myself, but it's hard to be confident when your product fails and you're trying to convince the people who saw it fail that you can build a business with it. Forget the cameras—I felt silly even saying the rest of my script to the audience. I wish I had just been more myself, because I should have made a joke like, "See, we really need that money so we can get our product to work right!"

Later, when the show eventually aired, we saw that they edited the footage just as I was lifting the device off the hair after the third stone should have been applied. It looked like they had just switched cameras. To the TV audience, it would look like it had been a success. But everyone in the studio audience, the ones who got to vote on who won the money, knew better.

Then Steve Harvey came over and asked me if it could bling anything. Not thinking about the device not working and trying to be funny, I said, "Yeah, we can even bling your mustache!" As soon as I said it I felt sick again because I knew we actually couldn't.

He thankfully didn't take me up on my offer and instead started joking around. "My wife and me are gonna be blinging everything. Blinging this and blinging that. We're going to have bling everywhere. We're gonna have a blinging party!" Everyone cracked up (it was much funnier than how I'm recalling it here), and that took the edge off me for the moment. None of that made it to the actual TV show though.

My competitors were two moms who invented Hose Hooker, a product you could stake into the ground to hold your garden hose. Steve Harvey had a lot of fun with that name as well, as you can imagine.

Once they finished explaining their product, we went to the middle of the stage to stand near that big cash-out button. I wanted to hit it. Though my product seemed much more unique and probably should have won, I felt my presentation, me this big-time saleslady, stunk. But at this point, my license deal was over. I needed money, and how would it look to an investor if I hit the button, cashed out, and took a lower amount? That I didn't believe I deserved even $10,000 for my product?

What kind of faith would they think I had in it and would they then have in me?

Neither of us hit the button, and it lowered back into the floor, my stomach with it.

Before we even flew out, the producers had asked me for an image of my product. I didn't realize it was so they could put it on the tablets the audience members were going to vote with, so I submitted a very plain image of the product standing up on its own against a white background. No Swarovski crystals, no logo, no gems in the hair, just the device.

Hose Hooker had sent an image of a dog playing in the water and practically smiling in the photo.

I wish my producer had suggested, "Hey, have a baby hold your product!" I think if I'd had a dog or a baby in my photo, I might have won. Mine looked like a baby. An alien baby. It wasn't giving anyone the warm and fuzzies.

I didn't win.

And really, Hose Hooker was a good product. The inventors were further along with it than me, and so they deserved to win.

The final score ended up being 49 percent to 51 percent. Before he announced that Hose Hooker won, Steve did say, "This is the closest it's ever been."

I had prepared myself that if I lost, I was going to be a good sport and not lose my decorum in the excitement of the moment. (Having ADD, these are things I must mentally prepare for.) I went right over to the Hose Hooker inventors to shake their hands and congratulate them. They did show that part on TV, which I was happy about. As a mom, you want your kids to see that kind of thing.

I wish we could have had a quick meet-and-greet with Steve Harvey after the filming, but after we lost, they rushed us off. I had bought my daughter a clear phone case cover that she was going to ask him to autograph with a Sharpie. I had brought his books too, hoping to get those signed. As a gift, I printed this quote on photo paper and put it in a frame for him:

> *"Man becomes great exactly in the degree in which he works for the welfare of his fellow-men."*
>
> **~Mahatma Gandhi**

I thought he'd like the quote, as he's worked hard to get where he is and has a gift for inspiring others. He's had many failures and times when others thought he was down and out, and so if you read his books, you'll see he's truly about helping others become successful. He knows how tough it can be to get there. I thought *Funderdome* made sense because of that, him helping entrepreneurs achieve their dreams with this show. But we never got the chance to get his autograph or a selfie, to give him the gift or even just thirty seconds to shake his hand and thank him for being an inspiration to others. I left the gift for him at the studio, but I doubt he ever got it.

After we lost, the producers separated Cambria and me and started yelling, "Don't talk to anyone!" Then they rushed both of us off, separately, but to the same room.

They later told us they wanted to capture our raw dialogue on camera. They wired us up with new mics and started asking us questions. We were directed to repeat the question and then answer it. I actually think that was the cutest part of everything we filmed. It was just us being ourselves, not following a script, answering questions in our charming, normal way. But they ended up cutting that part of the show too.

After that, they took us to another room, where we sat down with a psychiatrist to talk about how we felt about losing. He proceeded to play an animated video about being a loser, and how the animated character should be proud to be a loser. This little animated guy spent the whole video walking around making mistakes, breaking things, and talking about what a loser he was.

The psychiatrist was wearing an ascot and was very haughty, and he didn't seem to care about anyone. My Christian side was screaming, "Don't judge!" but it was hard not to with this guy. He explained that the video was to protect the psychology of the participants. We didn't feel that bad about losing until we watched the loser video. It was awful. I've tried to find the video just so I could show other people how horrible it was, but I can't find it anywhere.

Aside from the loser burn, I wasn't affected emotionally after the show. I actually felt great. Besides, I had been letting my emotions out that whole week. That's really how I am. If I'm sad, you know I'm sad. If I'm happy, you know I'm happy. And though I try to contain it somewhat with my kids and not share every feeling I have with them— they're kids, they can only process so much—it's not my natural state. I'm emotive.

But Cambria is pretty much the opposite of me. I've never seen her do this before or since, but when we got back to the hotel room that afternoon, she curled up into a ball and started sobbing. It occurred to me she had been overwhelmed. She'd been stressing about me, I think, maybe all week, and I didn't even realize how much emotion she must have been bottling up. In hindsight, I saw it all clearly. How I had been inadvertently dumping my fears on her. But she was so cool and seemingly fine, I had no idea she might have been twisting up inside and not letting it out, all in support of me and my dream. Me and my stupid dream. I was so mad at myself.

She had a total meltdown, and my heart broke. I felt so bad. God, I can be so selfish. My daughter had been there all week for me, listening to all my worries about the product, the script, the cameras. Keeping her cool. Cambria is truly an amazing girl. She'd been my champion, and now I needed to be hers.

I quickly went down to the lobby with her phone case and a Sharpie and found the shuttle driver. I asked if he could take me back to the studio. I didn't tell him, but I was going to track down Steve Harvey and get his autograph for her, come heck or high water. I would make it happen, no matter what it took, if I could get back on that set. But the driver said he couldn't take me back, and I knew there was no way to get past the guard booth in the parking lot unless I was on the shuttle bus. So I shared what I was hoping to do and asked if he could try to get Steve's autograph for us. He said he would try, but unfortunately, we got the phone case back blank.

Cambria was going to be fine though. And I reminded her that the loss was not really a loss—no matter what that crazy video said. I reminded her I would have paid to have had this kind of publicity for our product. It didn't matter if we won or lost. When the show was broadcast, we'd get huge national exposure. I told her we'd sell millions of Hair Blingers and that she had done an amazing job that week. She became more hopeful with all that, but really she just wanted his autograph.

We flew back home the next morning, her sleeping in peace on my shoulder and me with great anticipation. I was sure we were about to be launched in a huge way when the show aired, and I was determined to be ready when it did. I was not going to let God or my daughter down again.

Chapter 11

"Never confuse a single defeat with a final defeat."
~*F. Scott Fitzgerald*, Tender Is the Night

When we got back from filming *Funderdome*, I was feeling totally motivated. I told my kids this was the beginning of something incredible in our lives. I just knew it. My plan was clear. I was going to:

- Identify the problems with the ASTV-manufactured device.
- Look into buying the tool ASTV had made—I had an option in my contract to buy it for $25,000. I figured I wouldn't have to spend that much as they were out of the Hair Blinger business. It was useless to them, so I thought maybe I could pick it up for $15,000 or even $10,000.
- Find an investor.
- Work with the ASTV manufacturer or move the tool to another factory in China.
- Finally start manufacturing Hair Blingers.

Almost as soon as our flight landed, I got a call about being on another new show the Discovery Channel was doing called *Awesome Life*, with this billionaire Dave Yonce, who lived in, of all places, Oklahoma. They'd also found me by my failed Kickstarter campaign. (Hint, hint.)

The casting director, Kristina, explained that they were looking for people to manufacture their products at Dave's manufacturing plant in Oklahoma. I was over-the-top excited and knew this was a total God thing. Unfortunately, I couldn't take Hair Blinger on any other show within two years of filming *Funderdome*. But she really liked my personality and asked if I had any other products.

I thought that was very interesting. I said, "What? So you just want *me*? Doesn't matter the product?"

"Yes, we would love to have you on. Do you have anything else up your sleeve?"

It was funny and flattering. I actually did have another idea, something I still think people need (it's not a toy, more like a useful tool for the home). After I told her about it, she said she loved the concept. She told me she used to work for *Shark Tank* and that she'd never heard anyone have that idea before. I got so excited by that I started working on it in my spare time. Ha-ha! That lasted about two weeks.

I thought that was interesting that she was impressed with me and what I *personally* brought. That she would take me, it seemed, regardless of the product I represented.

And her surprise that she'd never heard of my idea before suggested to me that many entrepreneurs are unknowingly presenting similar concepts out there. It makes me think that if you can't stand out with your product, you should not discount standing out with yourself— and something about you that's unique. *You* might be the difference it takes to get the airing or the meeting—you might make for good TV, as they say. Maybe you're smarter than the other person with the same idea. Maybe you're working harder. Maybe you're further along. Maybe you're just nicer and not full of yourself—I can't tell you how many times I've seen arrogance trip people up in business.

Bottom line: you could be your own unique value proposition. Don't forget that.

It was neat to hear I might have something special to offer, including myself, but I had to stay focused on Hair Blinger and my children, the reason for my existence, and Arbonne, the business that actually paid my bills and kept us alive. Maybe I'll make that product someday. But, even now, I'm feeling it's time to take a break and just be Mom. I've worked hard since my kids were born—it's time. And we all deserve it. I only have my three oldest for a few more years as I write this. I don't want to miss a single day that I have left with them. And I need to make sure I've done all I can to have them ready to be thriving, productive adults out in the real world.

Though I couldn't be on the new show, I felt that me being from Oklahoma and that connection to this billionaire guy, Dave, might be for more than just being on the Discovery Channel show. He had a manufacturing plant in Oklahoma, after all. In the USA! I always wanted Hair Blinger to be American made. Maybe this was how it was to happen?

I needed to get in touch with him directly. How did I do it? You guessed it. I googled him. I saw Dave had a website and learned I could get a half-hour consultation with him for $200. I thought that was a deal. *What an opportunity!* Who wouldn't love the chance to get advice from a billionaire entrepreneur?

My dad did the play-by-play for OU football and basketball back in the day when Billy Sims, the Boz, Wayman Tisdale, and Bo Overton were there—yes, Bo Overton. If you were a girl in the 1980s and you knew OU basketball, you knew Bo Overton. We were all in love with Bo. Back to the main point: people know my dad, and so to add a little something interesting and to grab Dave's attention, I mentioned that I was John Brooks's daughter in my message. Dave messaged me right back saying, "Jiminy Christmas!" which is what my dad always hollered when OU got a touchdown.

Dave and I hit it off, and he did some mentoring with me, way beyond that half hour. He was great! He was also really interested in the product and talked to me a lot about manufacturing. Something he said that stuck with me was, "Once you have a product that works, launch it. Don't try to make it better and better, because you will always be trying to perfect it—and end up never launching it." He explained that you just run with the product as soon as it's good, and if you relaunch a version two, about 75 percent of your customers will probably upgrade and buy the new version. Your product has to work or do the intended job, of course, but it doesn't have to have every feature you've envisioned before you take it to market.

Now I felt like I had some real options with this connection. He introduced me to his head engineer, Billy, who understood my product right away and said, "Angie, my wife and daughter spend thousands of dollars a year on their hair at the salon. There is definitely a market for your product."

Although ASTV saw my product for older women, they were mainly targeting teen girls. I always saw the market being for women of all ages. Adult women to use for weddings, galas, or girls' nights out. Not something really for play, but more for adornment. Billy was one of the first men to see that too.

In November, I decided to reach out to Firm 2, whom I hadn't spoken to since ASTV took over the product. I wanted to tell them the exciting news about being on national TV with Steve Harvey and get some help with figuring out why the manufactured Hair Blingers didn't work correctly. I explained that I was almost out of money, but that I had the option of buying the tool and that I had a new American manufacturing contact.

Firm 2 offered to take a look at the production devices and give feedback on what was wrong. They too wanted to know why their design hadn't worked.

With my contract over with ASTV and my product about to be on national television, I was looking for help from people who either knew me or would be willing to work with me. I was running low on cash, and I was really feeling the pressure now to make it all happen. I needed an investor and the right people in place so I could move the product forward and quickly. They told us it could air at any time in 2017. What if the show aired in the spring? I started calling all my connections, looking for anything anyone could do to help me.

Firm 2 had contacts in China and said they could help me evaluate the tool ASTV had built, if we could come up with some terms. They said they could also help get Hair Blinger manufactured. Even if I did it in Oklahoma with Dave's team, they explained that it would be good for me to have an engineer on my side that I trusted.

After Firm 2 gave me their evaluation of the production device (essentially the Delrin shrinking, which I explained earlier), I understood it wasn't a reflection on their work, and I knew I needed someone to oversee manufacturing. I decided to offer partial ownership in my company if they would help me. I shared my goals and cash limitations—that I was sure were just temporary—and how big I knew this product was going to be. They weren't interested.

That was tough to hear. This was not because I wasn't used to being rejected, *LOL*. In sales, I could get a million nos and not skip a beat. This time it felt different to me. That they didn't share the confidence I had in this product, with so many opportunities popping up, surprised me. Did they not believe in their design?

"Gosh, that makes me think you don't believe in the product," I responded, and as I said, I don't usually react like that.

"No, no, no. It's not that," my contact told me. Then he gave me a whole explanation of, "This is just how we run our business. It's just a rule of the company. We don't get involved with our clients' business-es," and so on.

I offered equity into GEMC^2—Hair Blinger—to so many people, including my mom. I told her, "Instead of a loan, this could be an investment!" She wasn't interested. No one was interested.

I offered it to my new mentor, Dave, neighbors, friends, other investor connections I'd gained over the years. I was asking for referrals from everyone I knew. I had one friend who thought my idea was great and was ready to jump in with $30,000. I was so excited. We set a date to do the paperwork, but he never showed up. No call, nothing. I called him off and on for a few weeks after that but never heard from him again. And he and I had been friends!

It's hard raising money. Although I'd done it before, it seemed tougher now. Maybe the product seemed too risky or too far outside their wheelhouse. The bigger investors all seemed to want a tech product, not a plastic device for women's hair. And the smaller ones just didn't get it or want to come in.

I also offered equity to a handful of engineers along the way. Most just weren't interested in that kind of arrangement. Engineers are not entrepreneurs. I mean, they are willing to have their own companies and charge others for their work, but I don't see engineers as risk takers. I had some great talks with a lot of these smart guys, but they wouldn't invest, not even their time, for a piece of the action.

I'm thankful now that no one was interested, but at the time, I felt I just hadn't painted the potential clearly enough. Though I accepted I had more work to do—that's always fine by me—I didn't understand it. What weren't they getting?

It was one thing for *me* to be excited and talking about what a great product it was or would be, but I had validation from so many others by this point—and some who knew this space well. The ASTV company. ABC. The *Dancing with the Stars* hairstylists—every hairstylist I shared it with in fact—wanted it, especially for homecoming, prom, and weddings. The Discovery Channel. Not to mention we were about to be on national television with Steve Harvey. That alone seemed like a reason to jump in to me.

What about the dreams and God? Did that not mean anything to anyone? Are we that far from spiritual health, spiritual wealth? I know, I know. Keep it separate—keep God out of business. Mixing those two is a bad idea. We might stop using our minds as much and start using our hearts more. But business needs more love.

Whatever the reason, only God knows why, Hair Blinger wasn't clicking with people. I needed to do more for others to see it.

Thankfully, Firm 2 and I were able to strike a deal I thought was fair. They would do certain things to help me get the product development issues figured out, tooling analyzed, and just be my engineer on hand for whatever I needed for a $9,000 contract. I could pay this in increments—it just had to be paid within six months, basically by April of 2017.

I knew that I could put anywhere from $500 to $2,000 a month into my Hair Blinger business from my Arbonne business—God bless Arbonne—if I was careful with what we spent as a family. You know how it is—sometimes there was more month than money, but I was getting good at juggling it around and making it stretch when I needed to. I mean, at least one of my kids, if not all, ask me for something literally every single day. Not for hugs or kisses, mind you, just things. (Except Grace. She's still my little love bug.) Turns out though, I'm not only good at hearing no, I'm also good at saying it.

I signed the deal with Firm 2, and I was very appreciative.

It seemed to me I was on my way. I had a show airing on national television (have I said this enough?) so...

Marketing—*check.*

I had an engineer willing to work within my limited budget for the next six months, so...

Engineering—*check.*

I had a product that worked that just needed some fine-tuning, so...

Working product—*check.*

I had a tool in China I was close to owning to mass manufacture my product, so...

Tooling—*check.*

And loads of investors ready to jump in? Nope! So...

Money—*not checked*.

Still, I felt like my business was suddenly really *real*. I had always treated it as real, but now I had other components in place backing it up.

While I was working out my options with ASTV on the tool, Billy was quoting costs for manufacturing my product in the US and talking with Firm 2. Firm 2 was also connecting me to their China contact, who said they could send some guys to Shenzhen to analyze the tool for me, but it was expensive. I had to pay the factory $1,000 to run the tool for the day and another $1,800 to Firm 2's contact to send guys there to watch the tool being run.

Besides the money-raising front, everything else was coming together. I kept my focus on what I believed I had going for me. I didn't realize at the time that just because I'd filmed a TV show, it didn't guarantee my segment would air, so that wasn't a concern. Also, I was thinking like everybody else in America. If you're on national television, you're famous! Millions of people would be watching, which means we'd sell maybe five hundred thousand products, maybe a million. The sky was the limit. In my mind, I had leverage.

In reality, I didn't have any leverage. But I didn't know I didn't have any leverage, and that was the important part. Thankfully, God doesn't let us see the future, because if he did, most of us probably wouldn't get out of bed. We'd shore up, not realizing that the object of our desire was not the thing that would actually get us where we needed to go.

Then I got an email from HSN wanting to check out my product. I found out that out of the 150 products that were selected for Steve Harvey's show, only ten were selected by HSN, and mine was one of them.

That was it. I went to my mom and offered her whatever she wanted in return, any percentage, for another loan. I had already borrowed $35,000 from her by then. She asked me how much I thought I needed. I figured $50,000—which would cover buying the tool and manufacturing five thousand devices. My mom agreed to *loan* me another $50,000 at 10 percent interest. I knew it really wasn't enough, but it was enough to get me to a next better place. I'd figure out the rest when I got there.

This is one of the secrets to my success. I will make the next move before the 462 other moves after it are thought out. I'm scrappy that way. I'll take the chance of failing, looking dumb, and for it to be messy just to get to that next place in my business. Not conventional, but when you only have so many options and you believe in your idea, you do what it takes to make it happen.

I'm a risk taker, that's for sure, but I'm not a gambler. There's a difference. A risk taker bases the outcome on ability, while the gambler bases it on chance. I love rolling the dice, but the dice are grounded in my beliefs—my belief in God, my belief in myself, my belief in my dream.

With my trust in God, it's gotten way worse too. I never worry anymore. I know who's in control, so why not just run with it, work hard, pray a lot, and watch what unfolds? I have everything to gain and nothing to lose.

Practically speaking, I know it may not seem smart to some to run a business like this, but at the time, it was just me. No one would be hurt if it didn't work out—if I couldn't find an investor later. Not even my business would be harmed. It would, at worse, put things on hold temporarily until I found more money.

Plus, from the moment I got the money until the money ran out, I was going to be looking for more money—more investors, or at least *an* investor. I wasn't going to stop looking when the loan came in. You'll always need more money to get your business where it needs to be. It's not going to be twice what you think. It's going to be six, seven, maybe ten times more than you think. I needed to be prepared for the next step and to avoid unnecessary delays because I didn't have money lined up.

All you can do is control the controllables. I can't control other people, but I can control my effort, my time (mostly), where I spend my money (mostly), and my mindset (totally).

I know I probably sound like a wild card with all this, but that's what entrepreneurs are. We're dreamers. We don't count on luck, but we've put ourselves there, the place where and when the opportunity happens, so we can look lucky sometimes. But as entrepreneurs, we know otherwise. We work hard and have tenacity, and have just enough crazy in our makeup to know anything is possible. We believe in better things, and we believe in our part to make those better things happen. We are not there the moment it all comes together by chance.

What about you? Are you going to pursue what's in your heart? Are you going to run with the feather God's given you and make your dreams come true? I know you have an idea in your head. Or are you going to stay put? Just doing the same things you've always done but hoping your life will somehow change. Do you realize every time you watch an actor on television, you're watching someone who made their dreams come true? And what are you doing? Sitting there on your rear end eating chips. You have immeasurable gifts inside you, waiting for you to believe in them. Get off the couch, get off your phone. Focus on *your* dreams. We have one life—just this one. God is watching. Give him the story he wrote for you. He longs for you to live it.

Despite my entrepreneurial optimism, things were about to take a turn for the worse. About a week later, on December 23, Firm 2's contact reported back that it would cost more to fix the tool than to build a new one—and that a new tool would cost $80,000 and take forty-five to sixty days to build.

I crawled up into the fetal position and cried, and not on my bed but on the floor next to my bed. I guess I just felt that low. It hit me hard. It felt like I was back at square one. "What if the show airs in the spring?"

More than two years had passed since I had my dream. Not only did I not have a tool, but my product had too many parts. I didn't want to admit it, but I knew I needed a new design. My product was way over-engineered. But I didn't want to make that choice. Forget the sixty days for a new tool—a newly designed and prototyped device would take months to accomplish. I had a pivotal decision to make.

What I needed to do and what I wanted to do were not matching up. I wanted to plow forward with a finished product. I wanted to be past all this engineering product development stage. But I knew in my heart, in order to succeed, I probably needed to take some steps back and design a simpler device, a product with fewer parts.

After I pulled myself together, I went downstairs to the kitchen, and a plaque my daughter had given me months before caught my eye. It read, "God would have never put that dream in your heart if He didn't want you to live it."

I believed without a shadow of a doubt that he wanted this for me—it clearly said so in my kitchen. I knew what I needed to do—pray and turn it over to him. I let him know I was giving it back. The dream he gave me was his, after all. I sat down at the island and prayed.

> *God, you gave me this dream, and I don't know what to do now, which move to make, or if I even have a choice. So I'm giving it back to you. It's in your hands what happens next. I'm going to spend this Christmas, the birth of your son, in peace, knowing that all is good and that you've got this, me, us. Thank you for all you do in our lives. We're truly blessed. In your son's name I pray, amen.*

That was it. By the end of that prayer, all the stress was gone. I knew it was going to be handled for me. I could relax and enjoy my kiddos. We had a beautiful Christmas.

I'd love to say a miracle happened that week, and maybe it did, in a way, because I came back to Hair Blinger with more confidence than ever. I knew what I needed to do. I pulled a gut check, as my dad would call it (he did play-by-play for hockey too) and decided to redesign Hair Blinger. I called Firm 2 and told them I needed a new product design with less parts.

Right after New Year's, I got the oddest-looking concept back.

Not only was the device clunky-looking, but it also appeared to be awkward to use. It would be loaded with these little discs, my contact explained, "like Smarties candies," and each disc would have one stone on it. The discs would somehow slide into the device. Already it sounded horrible. Can you imagine women, or children, trying to pour these little discs into a tiny hole to load their Hair Blinger? Moms everywhere would hate me. It was a nightmare all around—how it was proposed to work, how difficult it would be to load, and how it looked.

New concept design proposed.

The "smarties" discs. Each would hold a single gem and be poured into the device.

Proposed tubes that would hold the individual gem discs and help to slide them in.

The *next day*, he sent me a bill for the full $9,000. He added thousands onto my current bill and listed it on the bill as "thinking" about a potential new design. Who bills extra for "thinking"? Isn't that considered part of the job?

Plus, it looked like he'd spent an hour on it, and he was charging me thousands of dollars. I was furious. Yes, me, a woman, a Christian woman at that, mad as all get-out.

The reason I say it like that is because I feel our first response when a woman is furious seems to be, to me anyway, to placate her and calm her down. Or judge her as irrational. Or to ask, "What's wrong with *her*?" If a man is furious, our first thought is usually more along the lines of "What happened to make him so mad?" So something done *to* him, not something *about* him.

Well, I was tired of feeling like I'm not allowed to be ticked. I let him know what I thought of his bill.

I felt taken advantage of. He'd told me in the very beginning, the first time I hired his firm, "Angie, let me give you some advice—don't tell anyone how much money you have." After that bill, I realized it was more like, no, just don't tell *this guy* how much money I have.

I was trying to keep my business alive, and he was trying to suck me dry.

Around this time, nicely, the owner of the ASTV company called me to see if I wanted all the devices they had made, as they were going to toss them. All I had to pay for was shipping. That would give me more than 250 production Hair Blingers. I said, "Absolutely!" I didn't know what I was going to do with them—they didn't work after all—but I couldn't imagine letting them be thrown away.

I realized later that what I actually got was something very valuable. In each box with the device was a pack of five strips, and each strip had eighteen five-millimeter Swarovski crystals on it. I hadn't even thought about the crystals being inside each box with the device. I had just gotten 22,500 Swarovski crystals with my glue on them! At that moment, I was truly grateful for unburned bridges. One of the best lessons on my journey.

How often in life do we have amicable splits? This is the only one I can recall in my life. (I'm joking, sort of.) Neither of us got what we wanted—they lost money and I lost time—but we didn't take our losses out on each other.

This is what business should be like and is probably the reason I like business so much—it's not so personal. As my ex-husband used to say, "It's show business, not show friendship." Established businesses know losses will happen, and the good ones are already set up to handle the losses. It's part of the risk of owning your own company. You just hope you have more wins than losses, or maybe that your wins are big enough to offset your losses in the end—because there are always more losses. At least on my journey it was this way.

Tip: don't burn bridges whenever possible. Figure out how to split up nicely.

Not all business is impersonal though. Primarily because businesses are made up of people. I still had a lot to learn and a ways to go.

Chapter 12

"Do not throw away your confidence; [for in due time] it will be richly rewarded."

~***Hebrews*** 10:35

Here we were again, back at the starting line. It was January 2017, and I was looking for an engineer to design my device. I didn't have a working prototype, working engineer, or working tool, but at least I had working capital and marketing in the form of a national TV show.

It's funny how quickly things can change, though. Just one month earlier, I had:

- An engineer—*uncheck.*
- A working product—*uncheck.*
- Possibly a tool to mass produce my device—*uncheck.*

Just another reason not to worry, because you never know what's around the corner. It could be good, like you hope, or it could be bad, like you fear. Worrying won't change what's coming. Worrying is about as useful as drawing a picture with a white crayon on a white piece of paper. (My son Christian gave me that line. Pretty cool, huh?) You're just spending time on something that gives you nothing in return.

Real problems in our lives are most likely going to blindside us on a random Thursday. Real rewards work this way too. It's all going to come together. Just do your part and let God do his.

My part was that I needed fewer parts. The device needed to be much simpler. It was overengineered, complicated to load, jammed easily, and it was too expensive to manufacture. The more parts it had, the more we'd have to charge the consumer. It had to be fewer than ten plastic parts. Period.

Though I was pretty sure that if I redesigned the product, I wouldn't be ready to sell anything when *Funderdome* aired, this was the decision I needed to make. Besides, I only had $50,000, so building an $80,000 tool in China was not an option. Even if I had enough money to build the tool, I still wouldn't have any left for them to run it and make the devices. Plus, the idea of putting all my money into a tool for a design that I knew wasn't ideal long term—for retail or the consumer—would have been a big mistake.

Sometimes the best decisions are also the hardest. Here's a huge tip I learned in this process: do what is best, not what is easy.

To create a device, each part has a price, and the more you buy at one time from the manufacturer, the lower the price per piece. We had eighteen plastic parts with our first design, with forty-four parts in all. We were looking at manufacturing a thousand devices, which gave us a cost of $14.24 per Hair Blinger, and that was before packaging, shipping, or duty tax, which would have added approximately $4.76 more. This put us at around $19 in cost. We wanted to at least double this number (ideally), to $38 wholesale, to make money and sustain the business. And that's what I wanted to sell it for retail!

That would have been fine if I sold it exclusively from my website. But to sell it wholesale to salons and other retailers meant they'd need to double my wholesale price. (This is a simplified version of how the numbers can work—you double what the manufacturer charges you, and the retailer doubles your number. This is called keystone.) When all factors were considered, Hair Blinger with the current design would have to have sold for around $80 each with the retailers. That was too high. It wasn't sleek enough, or simple enough to use, to warrant that retail price point.

MANUFACTURING TERMS

Here's a quick glossary of key terms you might want to know if you're thinking about manufacturing a plastic product in China.

- **Acrylonitrile butadiene styrene (ABS)**—the type of plastic used to make most plastic products.

- **Bill of materials (BOM)**—a list of every component necessary to make a single device. Not just the plastic parts, but also things like screws and springs. The BOM usually also lists the price per part.

- **Delrin (also called POM or polyoxymethylene)**—a stronger plastic than ABS and also more expensive, but necessary for parts that need to last longer and have less friction.

- **Gantt chart**—a project schedule for deliverables.

- **Free on board (FOB)**—an assessment that determines who has the risk and costs of shipping from one port to another. If it says, "FOB Ningbo" (a port in China), the manufacturer pays to get it to that port and loaded onto the ship. Then the client pays for the cost to ship it to a port in America, insurance, unloading, and shipping to the warehouse. The client also accepts the risk and expense should anything happen to the product while at sea.

- **Minimum order quantity (MOQ)**—the minimum amount a factory would agree to do in a single run on the tool.

- **Prototype**—a model made to test a product engineering design, usually made from plastic. A prototype can cost between $100 and more than $1,000, depending on the size and number of parts.

Besides having some capital, I also had all my manufactured Hair Blingers from ASTV, and over a thousand strips with Swarovski crystals on them. I felt I was in a strong position to get this right this time around. I confidently went back to Upwork, for the third time, to find a new mechanical engineering firm. Here is what I shared with potential firms after they signed my NDA, in our new request for proposal (RFP):

From Manufacturing & Company Standpoint

- Too many parts
- Tooling too expensive—$80K+ in China
- Too expensive: parts to produce (including $2 for assembly) = $11.82 + 3 strips (54 crystals) at $2.42 = $14.24 each before packaging, freight or duty
- Strip manufacturing/assembly difficult—especially for 3–4-millimeter crystals

From Consumer Standpoint

- Too complicated to load
- Only 18 crystals per load/strip (would be fine if simpler to load)
- Too expensive: $50–$100 retail with this design
- Backing plate not removable (or easy to remove)
- Removing strips from packaging a little tricky (never fully worked out)

Once I had narrowed down the list to five to seven potential companies, I sent each firm one or two production devices, which I thought was a great addition to the proposal process, because it gave potential engineers an opportunity to see what engineering had already been done—what worked and what hadn't. Also, I could do a video demo with the device and show the different aspects of what we needed, and I felt this made my communication much clearer this time. I also had engineering files I could share now.

I was feeling very confident. I figured these new guys would see the product as a worthy engineering endeavor and me, this serious client. I had already gone through the process of building a tool in China for goodness' sake. In my mind I was going to get better attention, better talent, and better results. This sounds good in theory, but sadly assumptions and outcomes don't always line up.

One of the candidates who applied, Troy Stevenson, wasn't the right type of engineer for the product, but he was smart and we got along great. He wasn't a mechanical engineer, but an aerospace engineer. And he hadn't worked with plastic designed products, but I didn't think these two things would matter. I mean, an aerospace engineer. He's basically a rocket scientist, right? I figured anything anyone threw at him would not be a problem. In hindsight, I would have been better with someone maybe less smart, but more experienced with plastic design and in the right field.

But coming off the heels of feeling like I had been taken advantage of twice now, I thought maybe I just needed an engineer of any kind—and a man—on my side. Plus, he seemed genuinely interested in me having success with the product and I really appreciated that, so I hired him as a consultant to oversee the job with me. He helped look over proposals and interviewed everyone with me. By the end of January, we narrowed it down to two potential engineering firms, Prospect 1 and Prospect 2. We made our objectives clear:

- Get the device down to fewer than ten parts
- Make it simple to load and use
- Identify the best method of getting the stones into the device, the carrier piece (currently the clear strips), and their manufacturability—which was going to be key

To us, the most important thing was figuring out how we were going to get the stones into the device—how they were going to be fed into it. Would we continue to use the strips Firm 2 had created, or would we need to come up with something new?

Second, and this was a question I'd had since the beginning, what machine was going to be able to mass produce these strips? To date, no one had been able to identify a process that could do this in large quantities and quickly. We needed a machine that could place glue on the back side of a tiny three-millimeter stone, then place that stone precisely in the center of a star cutout shape, fifteen to twenty times in a row, then do the next strip just as quickly.

To give you an idea of the enormity of this, if we sold ten thousand Hair Blingers, and each came with five strips with twenty stones per strip, we'd need to place glue on and precisely center one million stones. And ten thousand devices would be a small run. Most production runs had a fifty thousand minimum order quantity (MOQ)—that would be five million stones.

So I asked the new firms: Did it make sense to find a machine that already existed that was doing something similar to confirm this process was doable, then to design the carrier with that process or machine in mind? I felt designing the device should come second. We needed to figure out by what means the carrier (the strips) could be mass produced, we could then identify the machine and determine what kind of carrier we needed to make—whether to continue with strips or move to something else (disc, reel, etc.). Then, once we knew what would work best for the machine that was putting it all together (clear plastic piece, stone, and glue) we could design the device around that.

This made sense to Troy and me, and we considered it a key part of the whole development process of the device. There were really two items being designed, both equally important—the strip (carrier piece) and the device. We felt we needed to design it with the end in mind, starting with the strip.

Prospect 1 snickered when we suggested this was the tricky part of the development. They said, "Our manufacturing guy in China laughed at that. That's not a problem. That's easy." They sounded really confident, and that made me feel very excited.

In contrast, Prospect 2 sounded apprehensive, saying things like, "Well, I'm not sure" and "I'll have to talk to some people about that."

His proposal was similar to the other's in price, so his lack of confidence concerned me. In addition, he was a one-man team, while the other presented themselves more as a group, and with Chinese manufacturing connections, which Prospect 2 also didn't have.

Besides all that, Prospect 1 had found me on Gust.com, where I'd posted my pitch deck months before—not on Upwork. The week Troy and I were picking the engineer from Upwork, Prospect 1 had emailed me. We extended the deadline by one week to give them a shot at proposing, and I overnighted them a couple of the ASTV devices. When they were one of the top two prospects, to me, it was already a sign from God. Plus, when I first spoke to my contact there, he told me he had gone to seminary school. He also had a very unique biblical name. So you can imagine what all that had me thinking. Between those two things and this guy calling me out of nowhere, I had no doubt it was God's plan for me to go with this firm, and that my decision in December to start over with a new product design was preordained so that I could be with this group.

Adding to that, Prospect 2 couldn't give us a delivery date. He said it could take anywhere from six to eight months, but I knew I didn't have that kind of time. Even though we still didn't know when *Funderdome* would air, eight months would have put us in September to just have a working prototype. I was sure the show would air before then and I wanted to be manufacturing the newly designed devices by then. My goal was to ship when all the sales came in—or within a few weeks if possible. Prospect 1 assured me they'd have it done by mid-May, so at the end of January, we decided to go with Prospect 1. It was meant to be.

When we hired Prospect 1, who we'll call Firm 3 going forward, we expressed emphatically that the engineering of the device be done with the loading of the crystals in mind.

Troy asked Firm 3 to provide a Gantt chart, which I'd never asked for before because I didn't know something like that even existed. I was like, "Wow, we can just ask for these things and they nicely give them to us?" I knew I'd made a good decision hiring Troy. Between Firm 3 and Troy, I was sure we had an awesome team and we were going to make an incredible product. And we did!

I love the word *incredible*—it can mean good or bad.

Once they started working, we had to wait for them to send things back for my feedback. Then I'd clear up anything about what I liked or what I was expecting. I loved the look of the new design, but after a few back-and-forths, it seemed like they weren't doing much. Or they had hit a wall.

Then, after providing some non-working plastic models of their concept design, Firm 3 brought in a new guy as a third-party consultant. This new guy and I couldn't seem to get along, no matter how much I tried.

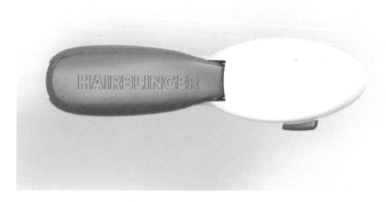

Concept for second design, Firm 3, February 2017.

He seemed to dismiss our concerns regarding keeping the parts count down and the importance of developing the product with the end in mind—the carrier piece. On one of our conference calls, he started telling me how I should be doing things—that I needed to have a better understanding of my cost projections and product manufacturing. He sounded just like the very first engineer who told me I wouldn't be able to make this product because I just didn't have enough experience.

Finally, when I'd had about enough, I said, "I really feel that's my place to decide." He was peeved and that was probably the beginning of the end of my relationship with Firm 3's consultant and probably with Firm 3, though I didn't know it at the time.

It's funny how women are perceived to be the sensitive ones, yet many of the male engineers I worked with seemed to get their feelings hurt quite easily. But instead of crying about it or lashing out, they were much more subversive and destructive. They would miss deadlines, be late for conference calls, not respond to emails. This caused more and more frustration on Troy's and my side. We spent so much time trying to figure out how to motivate them or get them to focus on my job; we really didn't know what the problem was—we found ourselves constantly analyzing them and making assumptions. They had all the power; they could take forever to develop the product, and what could we do about it? We were essentially at their mercy, growing more and more desperate to make them happy.

I was under the impression that in business we could talk straight and people wouldn't take it personally. Especially men. Maybe that sounds biased, but to me, it's all just business. I hire you, you do the job, I pay you the money, that's it. I'm the customer, you're doing your best to please me—not the other way around. Besides, we don't have to like each other to get things done, do we? Just do the work, people.

I didn't get yet just how wrong I was—or, more importantly, how this mindset could hurt me. I knew intrinsically with Arbonne that *no one* was working *for me*. I was the head servant leading a volunteer crew. And money only goes so far when it comes to job satisfaction. People are not robots. We're all feeling creatures that desire recognition and to be appreciated. Really, we all just want to know we're loved.

We said in Arbonne, people work harder for praises than raises. But I had not been applying this knowledge to Hair Blinger as much as I should have.

So I started to treat these guys as I would someone on my Arbonne team. With love, understanding, and gentle encouragement, hoping to motivate them. I think I even sent the third-party consultant flowers once. But this all became irrelevant. Firm 3's design was getting more complicated by the day. Troy was getting more worried. I was just still counting on God that it was all going to work out.

One day, my main contact at Firm 3 told me, "You know, Angie, many times we get jobs that seem complicated, but we figure them out pretty quickly. Then we get ones like yours, a job that seems simple, but is actually complicated." In the end, this was the only thing this firm said that carried any merit.

My main issue at this point with Firm 3 was that they assigned me to an outside consultant—a guy I didn't hire and who clearly didn't like me. The impression they'd given was they had a staff of engineers working on-site. My main contact said they'd had a meeting with several people about my job. Now I was being outsourced to a third party? It didn't make sense.

I eventually expressed my concerns to my main contact about the attitude and all the delays of the third-party guy, hoping he would also be upset and start having more oversight, but nothing changed. In retrospect, I realize that my main contact didn't care. It was as though he had moved on to other jobs, and whether mine ever got done or not didn't matter.

Internally the device was getting overly complicated in Troy's opinion, but what I loved about it was that it looked like a hairbrush. I thought that was perfect for a women's hair tool. But it might as well have been a real hairbrush that they were expecting to apply gems to the hair when all was said and done.

At the end of May, two weeks after the deadline of when the final working product was supposed to have been done, we were just getting a prototype that didn't work but was visually what they expected.

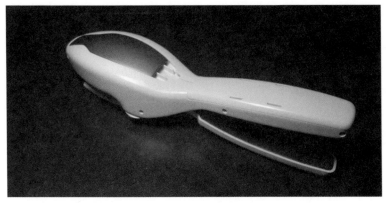

Non-working prototype of second design, Firm 3, May 2017.

After I reviewed it, I sent it to Troy. He called me right away and said, "Angie, did you know we're over twenty-two plastic parts?"

"What!" I said. I couldn't believe it.

"I opened it up and went over the CAD files," he explained. "The parts he has on here that are listed as aluminum on the bill of materials (BOM) are actually plastic parts."

When we addressed this with our main contact, he assured us that the parts were small and that the tooling would still be under $25,000.

After this, we requested a weekly call to ensure the work was proceeding now at a more focused pace. We actually thought they would care that they were weeks behind, but they started dismissing us on these calls, saying things like, "This is how this process goes." They became indifferent, callous, and even cold. Their attitude was essentially, "We're going to move however we're going to move. And you just hold on to your skirt there, missy."

By this point all but the final milestone payment had been made. We had little to no leverage. We were truly at their mercy.

One day, when I called my main contact to express a concern about a flippant comment the consultant had made in an email to Troy and me, he spoke nicely about it and calmed me down. He was strangely decent on that call, saying things like, "I know we're behind, but we're going to get it," and "Hang in there." By the end of the call, I felt reassured and I told him as such. Then, just before we hung up, he said, "I'm glad I could be a good counseling session for you."

Of course I'd already hung up when I realized what he'd said. I think I even thanked him after he said it. Wait, what? Counseling session? Was he serious? He thought I needed psychological assistance. *That* was the reason for my call? Not that I'd paid his firm nearly $15,000 at this point for a product that appeared to be way off target, weeks behind, and the outside consultant they'd hired to finish the job, because it was too complicated for them to do, had just insulted us? Heck, maybe I did need counseling. Someone sure did.

While all this was happening, let's not forget, I was still a single mother of four. All kinds of diversions, many hospital ones, unfortunately, were happening along the journey.

In the beginning of that summer, Christian's leg went right through a broken pool skimmer at an end-of-the-school-year pool party. He got a huge gash, all the way to the bone, on his shin. It was awful. It was the first day of summer too—he couldn't go into any water, ocean or pool, for six weeks. I felt so sad for him.

Later that summer, Cambria fell off a horse and broke her wrist. The whole thing was caught on video by one of her horse buddies. When she hit the ground, you could actually hear her say, "Ow! My wrist."

At the end of 2017, Evan tripped over a pillow and slammed his head into the windowsill. Cambria had to call 911 so that I could try to stop the bleeding and because I was panicked. There was blood everywhere, which freaked me out. Head wounds, I learned, bleed a lot. I followed him and my other kids in the ambulance to the hospital, and this wasn't the first time I was following an ambulance with sweet Evan injured inside and all my other kids with him. The scar ended up right above his eyebrow, so you can hardly see it now. That was good. And I hope this doesn't sound bad, but is a boy really a boy if he doesn't have some scar on his body? I know that's probably horrible to say but it feels true. I'm sorry.

One of the worst diversions was in the spring of 2015, right after the lice derailment, when we went to the pet store to get Evan a hamster— something he'd wanted for a good long time. He was holding one when all of a sudden Cambria asked, "Evan, what's wrong with your face?"

Immediately my heart skipped a beat. I looked down, and his whole face had puffed up. His lips were swollen and getting bigger by the minute. He had bumps everywhere. I knew he had a severe allergy to peanuts, but what was this about?

I yelled at the clerk, "Call 911!" and "Are there peanuts in the food you feed your hamsters?"

I got his EpiPen out of my purse as I ran out to the car for the Benadryl. I held him in my arms, sitting on the floor of the pet store, pouring Benadryl down his throat right from the bottle.

While we waited for the ambulance, Evan was crying and kept saying, "I just wanted a hamster." I felt so bad for him. All my kids rode with him in the ambulance to the hospital, and I followed behind them in my car, praying and crying.

When we went to the allergist a few days later, we found out he was not only allergic to peanuts, but he was also allergic to hamsters, gerbils, mice, rabbits, and cats. It turns out, the only rodent he isn't allergic to, because their hair is different, are rats.

What can I say? I'm that good "boy mom." I ended up getting him two rats. He named them Snowball and Spike.

For the most part, they're actually pretty cool, the rats, and they're much more social than the others. In fact, it's been shown they can actually die from loneliness. One night they started knocking everything over in their cage, including their metal food bowls. I didn't know this was the source of the disturbance at the time. I thought someone was downstairs robbing us, so I called the police.

After having lived on my own at this point for a few years, I was more confident with potential intruders, plus my kids were all there, so I felt safe—I mean, brave. I turned on all the lights and yelled down, "Hey, whoever is there, you need to leave! I've called the police! I've also got a gun and I know how to use it." I didn't have a gun. Those things will kill you. The noise stopped for a second and then started again. All my kids were behind me at the top of the stairs. I told them to go back into my room and lock the door.

When the policeman came, I let him in the house. There was still a ruckus in my kitchen, but it was dark. Then all of a sudden, I saw a man with a flashlight on my deck.

"There he is! Get him!" I shouted.

"That's my partner," he said, sort of laughing and sort of matter-of-fact. I guessed this wasn't the first time this had happened for them.

When we turned on the lights, we saw it was just the rats knocking over their food bowls. Those dirty rats!

In the summer of 2018, while at the beach with friends for the weekend, Cambria was riding a bike and the pedal swung around and gashed out half her calf and a piece of her ankle. She had to get twenty-six stitches. It looked like a shark bit her. That's what we say now, anyway, when anyone asks about the scar. It's impressive.

I honestly don't know how anything gets done. We're always getting sidetracked by something.

I try to do a fun trip every year with my kids. When Grace was just one, in the spring of 2015, I drove all four of them halfway across the country by myself to surprise my mom in Oklahoma for Easter. I looked up all the cheesy Americana things on roadsideamerica.com

I could and mapped it out to make it a fun road trip. We saw the biggest Rubik's Cube, stayed at the Peabody and watched Peabody's ducks on parade, stopped at Kooky Canuck and split a twelve-pound hamburger, and saw Luray Caverns and the Natural Bridge—two of America's natural wonders. We also visited the hotel where Martin Luther King Jr. was shot and of course the Oklahoma City bomb memorial. It's important to me that my children see the good and the bad in our history. Otherwise I feel I'm raising them in a vacuum, and how does that prepare them for real life? And by me introducing it to them, I can also be there to get them through the hard concepts of it and answer their questions. It also gives me a chance to share how my faith gets me through so much, and by this they might see how important it could be for their lives too. At a minimum I pray it will be a seed in their hearts and minds that can sprout and take hold someday.

That summer of 2017, while I waited for Firm 3 to deliver basically anything, I had decided to rent an RV and take my kids up to Niagara Falls and do some camping. I had originally planned it as a trip with just my kids and me, but my mom ended up coming too. I'd never driven an RV before, but it turned out I had a knack for it. I apparently have very good spatial awareness. I could back that thing up like nobody's business.

On that trip, something amazing happened. It was six days after Cambria's thirteenth birthday. I had gotten her, my mom, and myself necklaces with all these metal images stamped out in different shapes. One of them was a cross, with the word *faith* written above it. She held the necklace in her hands.

Cambria knew all about my faith and how much I really wanted to pass that baton on to her, to all of them, but I try not to push it. I think it's important they find it for themselves when it's time. I just let them know it's waiting for them. That someday I won't be here but God will always be here for them. And that he loves them even more than I do, if they can believe that. And I always tell them this with a big smile, like, "Isn't that amazing? He loves you more than me." Like, how is that possible?

I imagine this must say so much to them. I want them to know it's real and he's waiting to have a relationship with them, whenever they're ready. In the meantime, I continue to do my best to model what being a good Christian looks and acts like. I don't always succeed in this, but as my faith grows, I pray I'm becoming better at this for their sake.

She said, "How could I be holding this necklace, with this word on it, if it wasn't real?"

That was it for her. She was holding "faith" and then she had it, just like that. She started bawling. It was beautiful. It all happened before my eyes.

We celebrate that day every year now. What's really cool about it is that she found her faith on July 17, 2017, and I found mine on February 12, 2012. I have always felt intrigued by numbers and their meaning in my life. I believe God knows this about me and gives me confirmation many times through them.

The downside of the trip was that I spent a lot of it working.

Earlier in the spring, I had been looking for a firm that could help us with social media advertising and other marketing items. I emailed this cool company I happened upon online, Sling Shot. They were too expensive for me, but they nicely forwarded my email to their sister agency, Swimming Duck in Texas, owned by Gordon Law. Gordon is the nicest man, and he was excited about my product.

That summer, Swimming Duck introduced me to Jason Ward, whom they contracted with often, to help me get some good graphic materials for my website. Jason lived in Oklahoma and so of course, we hit it off right away. Jason is a Christian man with a beautiful family, as well as a talented artist and photographer, but originally a good ol' Kentucky boy, with a rough-and-tough hillbilly side. He had this whole dichotomy going that of course I related to and loved. We had many a laugh about him being picked by Gordon to be involved with this frilly girly product.

Jason worked with me to create a better logo and to get some good ad content. He was awesome and so much fun to work with and now a good friend of mine.

Fourth logo.

By this point I was pretty sure I wasn't going to have a product ready in time for the show, so I was going to have to do another Kickstarter. If you remember, with a Kickstarter you don't have to have your idea or product finished. You just have to give the backers enough confidence that you will fulfill their order eventually and hope they support you. You are free to ship their order a year or more later if need be, and the backers understand those conditions.

This time, I was going to set the Kickstarter goal for $10,000 and I was determined to reach it. Surely I could raise that much, but I wasn't going to chance it.

Jason really wanted to help me. He knew I was struggling and that I could barely afford what Swimming Duck was doing for me. He wanted to get me more than just a great new logo and some cute ads, but also some good video for my third Kickstarter that I'd launch when the show aired. I was still confident the show would be the thing that propelled this product into the stratosphere.

We were going to be filming my third Kickstarter video right when we got back from my RV trip, the last week of July—hopefully with a prototype that worked.

I had originally thought I would fly Jason out and we would film in Delaware, but he preferred to film closer to home in Dallas so that he would have all his equipment. I was fine with that, but what I learned on my vacation was that I was going to be responsible for getting all the models, makeup people, and hairstylists, booking the salon, and a million other details for the shoot myself. In Dallas—where I had zero contacts. Somehow in the planning I had missed this important piece of information. I ended up on the phone the whole vacation coordinating everything, while my mom had fun with my kids. Argh. It ruined my trip. I had been so distracted, in fact, that I only realized weeks later that the only group picture we had was with my mom and my kids in it—not me. It was like I wasn't even there.

I got an Airbnb in Dallas, which worked out great for parts of the shoot. We all had a place to stay and could use the house to film in. When we shot the videos, I learned that Jason's really a perfectionist, which made it stressful for him because this was my first shoot to co-ordinate and I had literally thrown it together in a week while driving a four-ton RV up the Eastern Seaboard with four children in the back. It got worse, as nothing went that smoothly or as planned. The models I booked didn't show up or didn't look quite like their pictures. Then the salon canceled, so I was scrambling to find a new one. It was unraveling by the minute.

Firm 3's "working" prototype arrived in Dallas the day before the shoot. Cambria was so excited. She loaded it and started blinging away with it, and it worked for like the first strip or two. Then it jammed. It wasn't her fault. They don't make the prototypes all that robust, and this one had many more issues than that—like *hundreds* of internal parts, for one. It did show us a huge problem with the design though.

The engineers had designed it without a way to open it up to unjam it. We had to do all our filming pretending it worked.

While in Dallas, I learned my episode of *Funderdome* was going to air on August 27. It was already the end of July, and we were nowhere near ready. Things were looking bad, and they were about to get worse.

Working prototype of second design, Firm 3, July 2017.

Chapter 13

"But I press on that I may lay hold of that for which Christ has also laid hold of me."

~*Paul*, Philippians 3:12

I don't know how I managed during this time. I can still feel the angst like it was yesterday. Prototyping the product is an important and necessary step *before* going to manufacturing. You don't want to work out issues after you've spent $30,000 or more on tooling. Most companies will do several iterations of the design and make five or more prototypes before even considering building tools. Large companies will sometimes make hundreds of prototypes before tooling. Anyone who knows anything about manufacturing would know that, yet Firm 3 didn't seem to know that.

In early August, I got an email from Firm 3 stating that they hadn't received the final payment yet. I was confused. After filming in Dallas, we sent them a list of over fifteen items that were wrong with the *first* and only "working" prototype. When I inquired, they said that whichever manufacturer I went with would resolve those final issues. They wanted to be paid in full though they hadn't honored their end of the agreement. This wasn't counting the twenty-two plastic parts it had—which was a whole other default, almost twelve more than they had been contracted to do. That is not how it's supposed to go. It was reprehensible of them to ask for final payment when they hadn't actually produced a working prototype.

Firm 3 felt that they had delivered a viable device. As I mentioned, it worked for those first one or two strips, but as soon as a gem got stuck inside, it stopped working. You had to unscrew it and take it completely apart to remove the stone or stones that were jamming it. We weren't even able to do this at the shoot, since it required several screws to come out. That wasn't going to work for the consumers, and it wasn't going to work for me. What, were we going to include a tiny screwdriver and tweezers with the instructions? "When your device jams, simply unscrew these eighteen screws and, as delicately as possible, pluck out any stones jamming the works"?

He said, "It does work. It's not our fault that you didn't ask for a way to go inside to unjam it in your RFP. That's additional requirements and features, and more money, if you want it to do that."

Really? Oh my goodness.

I did ask that it was fewer than ten parts—what about that small requirement?

It was time to say goodbye to Firm 3. I couldn't believe it. It was August, and I still didn't have a working prototype.

Unfortunately, just because someone says they're a Christian doesn't mean they have integrity. But don't let that be your excuse to judge an entire group or not find your own belief in Christ. Don't risk your eternity over one bad experience—even a million. Christians are people, and people can let us down. People can get it wrong and will, Christian or not. Besides, God didn't ask us to follow Christians. He asked us to follow Jesus. Don't put your destiny in the hands of man.

And even if it's God's will, it doesn't mean it's going to go well. He may have reasoning that won't make sense to you. I don't think it was a mistake that I went with Firm 3. God used that experience to teach me some lessons, and by making it another struggle on my journey, he gave me an even better story to tell. Always trust in God's plan and his timing. I think if you do, you'll see it makes sense in the end.

"He has made everything beautiful in its time."
~Ecclesiastes 3:11

I had to let Troy go at this point. He hadn't done much to make things go better or even for the product to be made to our specifications. He couldn't, though. We were both at Firm 3's benevolence—of which they had none. Troy even offered to work for free the last few weeks, but I didn't feel comfortable with that. He was so nice. Unfortunately, it all just ended without either of us feeling like we'd accomplished even one part of our goal. I know he felt bad, but it wasn't his fault.

Receiving Firm 3's request for final payment was a good indication that they weren't going to finish the job, and they confirmed that in an email soon after. Fortunately, I had already started talking to another engineer who was interested in helping me to make their device work. I found this firm because I got a Facebook message from a friend who had filmed on *Funderdome* with me in LA. Because of the timing of her message, it felt like another God thing. I had sent her a congratulations note—hers was the first *Funderdome* episode that aired—but I didn't hear back from her until two months later, the exact moment I realized I had no choice but to find a new engineer.

We chatted for a while about her show airing and mine coming up, and she asked, "Do you have product?"

"Almost," I told her, but then shared how my "working" prototype had issues. She told me how much she loved the guy she was working with, and how he got her product redesigned in less than six months. "He's phenomenal," she told me. "He's a little, you know, hyper. But he's really good. I think he's a genius."

So, I decided to ship my prototype to this new engineer. I told him about everything I'd been through up to this point, and the date my show would air. He told me that he had his own manufacturing plant in China, and that his engineers were going to figure out all the problems with my design and make it work if I went with him.

"I'll put twenty guys on it," he told me. "They can get all this done."

At some point I left a message for him, saying how nuts I was feeling about all this, like Einstein's definition of insanity: "Doing the same thing over and over again and expecting different results." I ended with, "How is hiring you going to be different from the last three guys I hired?"

When he called back, he told me, "What you said made a lot of sense, and not many things make me stop and think like that. I was really thinking about that message for about thirty minutes before I called you back."

My kids were more involved now than ever before, especially Cambria, and when I expressed how unhopeful I was that this time would be any different, she said, "Mom, like you always say, what good are low hopes?" I love when my children repeat my messages back to me. Who knew they were even listening? It's a wonderful reminder that maybe I wasn't all that bad at my first and most important job—being a mom.

This prospect sounded more likable and a lot less stuffy. He was clearly different from the other engineers I'd hired. He sent me a photo of himself holding this huge Nerf gun, arms covered in tattoos, wearing sunglasses, and he had a goatee. He looked young. He said he had a 180-plus IQ, and I believed that he was this genius, maverick engineer who also seemed to care for people. He told me he was a "force of nature," and of course I loved that. We went back and forth for a few calls. I did a three-way call with him and another company owner, who also sang his praises.

In early August, he sent back a video with a quick high-level analysis of Firm 3's "working" prototype. He said he'd already identified 85 percent of the issues, and it wouldn't be a problem for him and his factory guys in China to fix them.

On our phone calls, he talked really fast, but in a confident "I'm busy but I'm making time for you" kind of way. It was exciting to talk to him, and I was feeling grateful.

When we began discussing terms, he said, "Look, I will guarantee you Christmas. But you've got to give me everything you have up front, because I'm not gonna be nickel-and-dimed along the way if I'm going to deliver this so fast."

I was okay with that. I mean, I was a start-up, after all. I'd been juggling funds now for three years. I'm fairly sure most start-ups are like this, scrambling for money. It's half the battle of having a successful business—finding the funds to keep it alive. Of course he worried about that. It made sense to me. But I was still nervous. His proposal was so simple, it was two paragraphs at the bottom of an invoice (and there was even a mistake in one of the paragraphs).

For the record, I normally don't give someone all my money, especially with such a weak two-section agreement. I didn't even share it with Glenn, because I didn't want him to delay things or to think I'd become a blinging idiot. I decided to trust my instincts and have faith in my friend's glowing recommendation. Christmas was such a lure for me too. I was going to be on national television, and I could promote that when the millions of TV viewers came to my Kickstarter or website. Plus, we only had a little over four months till Christmas, so there wasn't time to think. I needed to move. Tip: never do this.

He also told me that if he didn't hit Christmas, he'd take $1,000 off the manufacturing of the product each day he was late in delivering.

On August 9, I signed the tiny agreement and wired him, my fourth engineering firm, all the rest of my money, a little over $17,000.

Now usually when you hire someone, you start communicating right away. One of the worst things you can do to a customer is to get the sale and then disappear. These are the salespeople people can't stand—do anything for you, take a zillion calls and texts for the sale, but then barely get back to you after they get your money or the deal. You can tell a good engineer if they're following up with you immediately. They need your input, and now is the time to confirm all the communication that happened preagreement. Firm 4 had told me it was his birthday the next day so he wouldn't be working, so I wasn't worrying that this didn't happen. (When I shared this with my editor though, she said, "What is he, ten years old?")

The day after his birthday, on August 11, he was scheduled to meet Jason in his hotel room at Choctaw Casino in Oklahoma to film some more shots we needed for the Kickstarter. Jason was going to film some models getting their hair blinged at one p.m. Then he would film Firm 4 speaking about the engineering aspects from two p.m. to three p.m. After that, Jason was going to rush out and get set up at a ballet studio to film there by four p.m.

It was a tight schedule, but it looked like we had it all lined up nicely. However, that morning, neither Jason nor I could get ahold of Firm 4. We both kept calling and texting his cell phone all morning. I knew Firm 4 was checked into the hotel, because they connected me to his room when I called, but he didn't answer there, either. Jason had a truckload of stuff—lights, lenses, tripods, all his equipment that he brings to his shoots. They were supposed to meet at one p.m., but the guy was nowhere to be found as Jason and the girls stood outside the hotel. Jason needed the guy's help to unload the truck, plus just to be let into his room to get set up and do the shoot.

Finally, around one thirty p.m., he responded, and he seemed annoyed. But I was so relieved that he was alive. *Everything is fine again,* I thought, though a little red warning light was flashing in my head.

Jason called me when he made it back home that night, around ten p.m. "Oh my gosh, we need to talk," he told me. He sounded really worried and stressed. "Are you sitting down?"

Jason is a straitlaced no-nonsense kind of man. He was still in shock when he shared with me what all had happened that day. When the guy from Firm 4 finally met up with Jason, he had a Bloody Mary in his hand. While Jason and he were trying to move Jason's equipment from outside the hotel to inside the lobby, Firm 4 spilled his drink all over some of Jason's equipment.

Jason told me that he said, "Dude, put your drink down," but instead the guy just tossed the whole thing, glass and all, right into the trash can.

When they got up to his room, Jason saw the guy had anywhere from $10,000 to $15,000 worth of poker chips on the bed. Then Firm 4 started bragging about how he's this professional gambler and he wins all this money and all the casinos put him up in suites. Was my entire product development fund that I just wired him two days before sitting on his bed in the form of poker chips? Had I just given the last of my money to a drunk, clumsy gambler? I thought he was this cool, eccentric engineer. Jason felt bad for me, and I felt sick.

It went from bad to worse. Over the months we worked together, he would yell at me when I'd ask for updates. I walked on eggshells the entire time I worked with him. He always had an excuse if he missed a call or a deadline. First, he got the time difference wrong. Really? From Texas to Pennsylvania? It's an hour. What happened to the 180-plus IQ? Then he was deathly ill. Then food poisoning. Then a car ran over his phone. In the middle of conversations, his phone would die, and I wouldn't hear back from him for days. It was always something. I had gone from horrible with Firm 3 to a living nightmare with Firm 4.

Cambria was getting more and more mature and saw my frustrations with Firm 4. She told me, "Mom, you need to give him a chance. He's guaranteed it for Christmas. That's months from now. Give him some room." She was the voice of reason that kept me from flipping out on him a few times that year.

Though Jason's call concerned me, I had so much hope for what my TV appearance was going to do, I wasn't too worried. I figured once we aired, things were going to take off and nothing would be able to hold the product back.

On August 21, the day of the solar eclipse, six days before the show aired, I launched my Kickstarter. We had an awesome video, and our landing page had so much great and clearly worked-out information. We looked sharp. We were ready for the tidal wave.

In the midst of all this, I seemed to have thought it would be a good idea to chair one of the biggest fundraisers at my daughter's school, held every year at the beginning of the school year. Why do we do this to ourselves? I guess I hadn't yet found the grace and the strength to say no. At least not to volunteering.

I do love entertaining, and to put on an event like this, tapping into that creative side of me, is fun and exciting. We did a great event and raised a little over $14,000. However, a couple months later, just after I was complimented on how great that fundraiser was, I was asked to chair the eighth-grade dance too. Apparently, flattery gets you everywhere with me, because I agreed to chair that event too. Finally, after that dance, I found my graceful *no* strength. If you're a mom who needs it too, just chair two events in the same year. You'll get it!

The night we were airing on *Funderdome*, we held a viewing party at my house. This was the moment, the big marketing moment I had been waiting for and counting on for nearly a year now. I was so excited for what I was sure was about to happen. The party was fun and I was happy with the show—I hadn't seen any clips or knew what footage would be in it or cut until that night.

Jason and I had prepared a speech for the livestreaming segment to share at the end of the show. (Jason is a writer too. Just another of his many talents.) Only he—as a consultant with my company—my mom, and my children knew we hadn't won. I felt bad not telling other friends and family when they asked. They all assumed we had won, but I couldn't tell them, because my contract forbade sharing the results before the show aired. Jason and I wanted to put the loss in a positive light as we felt it should be. Here's what we wrote:

I'm both thrilled and humbled for all of you who watched our episode and who are joining us now live! My dream is to be going out to dinner and look over and see a stranger with bling in her hair. Can we really make ripples in the fashion industry? Will girls bling out their hair before a pep rally at school for a little extra school spirit? Will ladies add some bling before going out on a girls' night out? Will this become a must-have for brides in the coming years? Could we see our looks being talked about in all the bridal magazines? What about prom and homecoming?!

I can't think of a better season coming up for Hair Blinger to make a splash. But we really don't have to even wait that long. With your help, we could get Hair Blinger to be the stocking stuffer for all women in 2017! You could be the trendsetter at your school, in your cheerleading squad, dance team, ballet studio, drill team... the list goes on and on. The exciting thing is we've created the hair tool to do this. What you create with that tool is completely up to you! I can't wait to see how you girls will use Hair Blinger to create your own styles.

Sadly, we got very few sales from the show. When I saw we weren't selling millions of Hair Blingers after *Funderdome* aired—yes, the ASTV owner had been exactly right—I wondered if we could even sell $10,000 worth of Hair Blingers. I decided I needed to blow it up myself somehow and bought all these email addresses, a little over a hundred thousand, I think, and did a huge email marketing campaign. The guy who sold them to me was really nice and said, "You'll hit it with these."

I didn't get anything from it that I could tell, and I reached out to him about it.

"You didn't get anything?" he asked.

"No."

"Hold on," he said, and he went and checked out my Kickstarter. As he was looking at it, he said in a questioning manner, "Your Kickstarter hits every box. There should be no reason this isn't getting funded. I don't get it."

We had been on national television, I haven't even mentioned that Nickelodeon discovered my product and did this whole cute video and posted it on their Facebook page, and now one hundred thousand emails generated nothing. What was I doing wrong?

Around that time, I read some passages in the Bible that said God will hide you if he doesn't want you seen at that particular moment. He will hide you in plain sight. That struck a chord with me. It reminded me that it's going to be how he wants it to happen and on his timing:

> *For He will conceal me there when troubles come; He will hide me in his sanctuary. He will place me out of reach on a high rock.*
>
> ~*Psalm* 27:5

> *You hide them in the secret place of Your presence from the conspiracies of man; You keep them secretly in a shelter far from the strife of tongues.*
>
> ~*Psalm* 31:20

I decided I was going to have to fund my Kickstarter the old-fashioned way, by getting on the phone and badgering all my friends. Sometimes people don't realize when we're down. We think they do, but they won't many times unless we reach out. Your family and friends love you and want to help, but they're all living their own lives and think you're doing okay if you don't let them know otherwise. I understood this and so knew that I had to start calling them, one by one, not just posting on Facebook, and let them know how much I needed them.

One of my friends, Jeni Bufano, asked, "Angie, what's wrong?" when I called her.

"Oh, nothing. Why?"

"Because you never call me, so I was worried."

We never did call, just text, Facebook, or see each other at the school. She ended up buying five Hair Blingers! Love her!

Since my third Kickstarter wasn't doing what I thought it should, I also started spending a lot more time on it than I had planned. I was researching what had worked for others—email marketing, landing pages, backer clubs, cross promotions. You name it, I was learning about it and doing it. I worked that whole campaign, weeks, doing whatever it took just to hit $10,000 in sales. And I was spending zero time with my kids. But with all my work, we were still over $2,000 away. Nothing was working. It occurred to me he might be at work.

Here's what I posted on Facebook on September 17, 2017:

> *So here's my dilemma... My Kickstarter hasn't fully funded and there are only 3 days left, so my temptation is to disappear into the basement and have my oldest children watch my youngest children (as I've been doing lately) and figure out how to do a FB ad the "right way," email contacts I haven't reached out to, harass those of my friends who haven't ordered their Hair Blinger yet (I know they love me—this is what I keep telling myself anyway), or spend the afternoon with my children and trust God to handle this (knowing I will work hard Monday and Tuesday to hit our goal because I just can't let down all the supporters we have already).*
>
> *This morning I was sure I was going to spend the afternoon with my kids, because at church this morning they spoke clearly about how without him we can accomplish nothing. But then I saw a couple of messages and emails after church about our project and fear took hold again. And I decided I would spend*

the whole day working, but it wasn't settling right on my heart. So I sat down to spend some time to pray about my dilemma and look into my questions about where we are and why we haven't blown up as everyone predicted and expected and even still messaging me that they're surprised we're not way past our goal actually... and this is what I read:

"Do everything in dependence on Me. The desire to act independently—apart from Me—springs from the root of pride. Self-sufficiency is subtle, insinuating its way into your thoughts and actions without your realizing it. But apart from Me, you can do nothing: that is, nothing of eternal value... Use your freedom wisely by relying on Me constantly." [Jesus Calling, Enjoying Peace in His Presence, *September 17—an amazing book I go to often for daily devotionals.*]

And that was what I heard at church, but I thought I can work on all this today, it's just one Sunday afternoon after all with my kids, right? They'll survive and probably won't even remember this day a few weeks from now. But I'll know the choice I made. And how many Sunday afternoons like this will I have? Where they still like me and think playing with Mom is awesome. And in practical matters, they're at their dad's next Sunday, and then the following Sunday, who knows what may be going on and then all of a sudden, Cam is 14 and not 13, Christian is 12, Evan 10 and Grace 4. Not the age they are this Sunday, today. And if I choose work over them today what does that say about my faith? What does that say about my trust in him who I call my Lord and Savior? And how can he have the glory if I claim all the work?

We had over 200K views from our Nickelodeon video they did, over 100 shares and 100s of likes, but not one pledge that we're aware of from it, so if that doesn't tell me he's in charge, I don't know what does.

"You will not find My peace by engaging in excessive planning, attempting to control what will happen to you in the future. That is a commonly practiced form of unbelief. When your mind spins with multiple plans, peace may sometimes seem to be within your grasp; yet it always eludes you. Just when you think you have prepared for all possibilities, something unexpected pops up and throws things into confusion. I did not design the human mind to figure out the future. That is beyond your capability. I crafted your mind for continual communication with Me. Bring me all your needs, your hopes, and fears. Commit everything into My care. Turn from the path of planning to the path of Peace."

So I know I can't carry this or take this all on my own and am pretty sure I never have—even though I have felt that way many times on this journey. This was his dream after all for me to do and so today I leave it all to him.

And I'm gonna go play with my kids!

That last line still makes me cry. I don't remember what we did that day, but I do know the choice I made. And he does too.

The next day, a Monday, I saw an email that had arrived the day before that was going to change my children's, my, and Hair Blinger's future forever. It was from a toy company that was interested in licensing my product. They said it was the second time they had reached out to me, but I never saw their first email.

If I hadn't made the decision to trust God, to fully believe he had me that Sunday, would I have seen the second email?

He wants to know we're ready to do our part, and he does test us, only so that he can know he can trust us. "To whom much is given, much is expected" (Luke 12:48). You may think no one's there, that you're all alone, but I'm sorry, you're wrong. And since he's the only one who matters, we have to trust him by doing the right thing, not just the thing you want to do, and by doing so, you show him he can trust you with greater things.

I emailed the toy company, and they called me right away. "I saw your product on *Funderdome*, and we'd love to talk to you about it."

Chapter 14

A couple of days after my Kickstarter ended, my engineer at Firm 4 called me. By this point, he'd supposedly been working on my prototype for two months, but he was hardly communicating with me, so I really didn't know what was going on. When I saw it was him calling me, I nearly fell over a chair as I leaped to grab my phone.

"I've got good news and I've got bad news," he told me.

The bad news was that his manufacturing team in China couldn't get Firm 3's prototype to work. But the "good" news was that he wasn't going to charge me more money to come up with a different design.

It took him two months to determine this? I started thinking about how Firm 3 had told me that, whichever manufacturing factory I went with, they would get it to work correctly. Ugh. *Here we go again*, I thought. *Just the same ole thing.* Though Firm 4 said this was the good news, it had always been my understanding that he'd make the prototype work or make a new design. Maybe he waited to see if my Kickstarter worked so he could charge me more to make a new design if it had. I was fairly paranoid at this point, and trusting an engineer to do anything they said was pretty much over.

I wasn't sure how to take this, except to be...grateful? I mean, I didn't have any money, except from our Kickstarter, but those funds needed to be carefully preserved. I didn't have any other option but to work with him, so I thanked him and asked, "What about Christmas?"

"I still think we can hit Christmas," he said.

That line really makes me laugh now.

Kickstarter showed we'd surpassed our goal of $10,000, with $10,509 raised. But $1,440 of that did not process. We only really raised $9,069. Then Kickstarter got 5 percent of that and the bank got their share, leaving us with $8,314.63 in total. I had sold 169 devices to 131 actual backers, sixty-five of whom were friends, and all expecting their Hair Blinger for Christmas, especially the sixty-six backers I didn't know. I had to keep hopeful, and I was. What good are low hopes, right?

I had a call with the founder of the toy company who had reached out to me and learned they were interested in licensing my product. I arranged to go in and meet with them the following week. I had told them that I would most likely have to manufacture my product with Firm 4. They were interested in seeing my agreement to see if they could get me away from him if they felt that was necessary. While I was walking into their offices, I was thinking, *I'm gonna do a deal with this company.* I felt it was clear. I needed more and bigger resources to make my product—and this company, an established toy company, was it. I was sure of it.

I didn't win *Funderdome*, but that show brought me to here. Every failure is simply a deposit into your business. It comes from effort, and effort is work, and work is what it takes. Don't focus on the outcome of the effort or you might get discouraged. Just keep making deposits into your dream. You'll eventually get to draw from it.

I waited in the lobby for a while before the founder of the company came out to greet me. He escorted me into their conference room, which was lined with all their products. I was amazed. I knew this brand well—everyone did. I played with many of their toys when I was a kid, and my kids played with them now.

Within a few minutes, others joined us in the conference room, including an engineer, a product specialist, a marketing VP, and the CEO.

During the meeting, we talked about some of the history of the company and of my product. One of the biggest takeaways I got was that if I wanted to be on the shelves in time for Christmas *next* year, I needed to be at Dallas Toy Fair (at that time, it was called Fall Toy Preview) *this* year. I didn't realize this was how long the process took, but knowing this and about this show would be important later.

Getting toys to market all starts with Dallas Toy Fair. This event, in October, kicks off the whole season, all the way through to New York Toy Fair at the end of February. The amount of time it takes makes sense when you think about it. The retailers need to first see the new items the toy companies have come up with and give feedback—that's October in Dallas. Then the toy companies make changes to their products—the look, color, quantities, packaging—while shopping these new toys at other shows in Hong Kong and all over the world. They show off the revised products at New York Toy Fair in February, and then the orders start. Shipping happens between March and May. Testing happens on the shelves in June. I thought that was so interesting to learn—this is why you'll see a lot of toy ads on TV in that first week of summer. The metrics are measured, then the big orders are placed. In the third quarter (July through September) everything ships for Christmas.

They gave me another important insight into how to make a product successful. I learned when I explained our disappointment with *Funderdome* and the sales we received from it, or lack of sales, that TV's a wash unless you're in stores.

The founder explained, "You need TV ads. Distribution. And in-store presence. You need all three of these to make a product successful."

To have ads—that's millions of dollars. To have distribution— that's established connections and more money. And to be in stores— that's millions of dollars (in product and overhead costs). This may all sound simple, but if the money, connections, and team are not in place, it doesn't seem likely your one-man or two-man company will make it far.

I know there have been products that were better than mine but failed because they didn't have the money to spend on marketing. I know products that are not as good as mine that sold way more be- cause they blew up that side of the equation. It's a formula. I'm not saying quit and pack it up if you don't have these elements in place or the possible millions to put them in place. I'm just saying when you get close and the time comes to make a potential licensing deal, or to take on an investor who brings these kinds of funds and knowledge to the table, if you don't have all three ready to go on your own, take that deal.

The founder switched gears to Firm 4. "So this engineer guy is also helping her with the factory. He's basically saying, 'Hey, I'll do all the engineering. I own part of this factory in China.'"

He turned to me. "We know that's BS. We hear that all the time."

Then he addressed the others again. "He also told her, 'I'll sell you these finished' and 'I'll guarantee to have these units to you that work for your shipment in December.'"

Then he turned back to me. "That's BS too."

Though I knew all this was probably true even before hearing it said out loud, it was still disappointing. But I didn't have a choice. I had to believe in the engineer I'd chosen and support that path till there was another choice I could make. I'd given him everything.

At this point, I was just grateful for the possibility of working with a team like this. There wasn't one person sitting at that table in that room who had less than twenty years of experience with that company. They were about to become my heroes.

"Being that we use our own manufacturers, we control the price on the piece to make sure this is a $19.99 item," the founder explained. "This guy is going to charge her somewhere between seven and ten dollars, which immediately makes it a $29.99 to $39.99 item. We're going to read her agreement see if we can get her away from this guy, and then hopefully, we'll be able to do this with our people."

These guys were toy giants. They knew this business inside and out. I knew that not making a deal with them at this moment would have been reckless. I now had customers to think of. I pretty much agreed I'd license my product to them by the end of the meeting, even if that meant cutting my current engineer loose—it's not like he had done anything but scare me to death for the past eight weeks.

As we were all getting up to leave, I asked the founder if I could get a picture with him and the CEO. He said, "Absolutely," but I saw the CEO roll her eyes.

When I was younger, I used to get bent out of shape over stuff like this (BEICOM is ringing in my ear). To keep it from happening in the past, I'd gone overboard with my expertise on whatever I was presenting to make sure everyone in the room knew how much I brought to the table. But I didn't like this approach. It wasn't me. I like to listen, learn, laugh, take notes, capture the moment on film—ha-ha.

Another time, I was on a business call one day when my mom popped by. I said to the woman I was speaking with, "Hey, my mom just got here. Would you mind if I put you on speaker?"

My mom had loaned me $85,000 by this point, which made her a pretty big lender if nothing else in my company, and though the woman on the phone didn't know that, or that my mom was a smart businesswoman in her own right, she replied snidely, "Sure, I'd be happy to talk to your *mommy*."

So these things happen. Let it go. Think of it this way: if someone wants to make assumptions about who you are and treat you poorly, or like an idiot, understand that they're the ones with the problem. Acting without class or tact is their issue, not yours. Don't let anyone's jabs get in the way of you moving toward your goal. The best comeback is being successful. Ignore it and floor it! Your time will come.

I started doing that on this journey, being more myself. I met quite a few sharks, but I was determined to stay me—grounded in my faith, knowing God had me at the end of the day. I was free to be me. As it turns out, just being me became an advantage. When someone judged me because I wasn't fitting a mold, it revealed more about them and who they were. Apparently, my mannerisms, maybe my voice, maybe my giggle, gave way to faulty gauges of work ethic or intelligence. Not with everyone, but some. Don't get me wrong—I can do dumb things. Just ask my kids. But it's not like I'm completely clueless. I know that about me, and I know that about others.

I've stopped trying to tell people who I am. I've stopped trying to prove to everyone I'm smart and careful even though I might look loose and fast. I've decided instead just to be me and let things unfold more naturally. I used to get upset, thinking, "Don't people realize I'm smart?" Now I've stopped being defensive about who they think I am. Besides, what other people think of me is their opinion, not his, and shouldn't concern me.

When you start being you, a funny thing happens. You also stop judging so much when others are just being themselves. It's a two-way street. If I'm going to be me—accepted or not by others—it puts ideas in my head about accepting other people as they are too. Darn it. Seriously, though, I don't feel confined anymore and I don't want others to feel this way either. As I find more love for myself, I find more love for others. I give more people the benefit of the doubt. And I'm hoping the more I'm myself, and also successful, the more that will show others they can be who they are and be successful too.

There is no mold.

The less we judge and the more we treat everyone with love and kindness and compassion (that's a big one), the better our lives become. Others may not change one iota because of it, but you'll feel better and enjoy the journey a whole lot more.

The next day, during a follow-up call about the agreement, the toy company told me they wanted to display my product for potential retailers at Fall Toy Preview in Dallas, which was the next week.

Before this call, they had sent over their license agreement, which was even less detailed than my engineer's two-paragraph agreement. Their whole agreement consisted of one paragraph that was three lines, in like size thirty-two font.

Glenn was not going to let me sign that to save my life. And since this was a big company that could crush me, I definitely brought in my ace, Glenn. We were rushing and couldn't work out a clearer agreement in the short time frame, so he wrote up a letter of understanding, which was about eight paragraphs longer than what they had proposed for the whole agreement. His letter basically stated that they could take my product to Fall Toy Preview, but it listed a few stipulations, and that we would formalize a contract when they got back from the show.

When I say big companies can move quickly, I'm not joking. This toy company renamed Hair Blinger, developed packaging, and had created an entire brand—graphics and all—around my product, and within four days it was on their showroom floor. That was telling. How quickly they had done this was astounding to me. I never forgot it, and what they did that weekend would be a big influence on decisions I would make later, when it mattered.

They wanted to have the "functioning" prototype, working or not, in Dallas by the next Monday, the day before the show started on Tuesday, so their engineer and his guys could look at it and ideally fix the issues before it was demoed during the show to potential retailers. My engineer had sent the prototype to China, but we'd already started a rush to get it back to Dallas before I even met with the toy company. It arrived on Monday, and Firm 4 drove it over to their hotel Monday night. But it arrived in pieces, so he delivered it in a Ziploc bag. They couldn't demo it at the show—which probably would have been the case even if it had arrived put together, since it never worked.

The next day, my engineer called and said, "I'm not supposed to tell you this, but one of their people last night said to me, 'I'm not supposed to tell you this, but Walmart's interested in the product.'"

I was excited to hear that news, but I was also nervous about him being there without me. I knew they were possibly going to attempt to cut him out of the manufacturing part. But when I asked the CEO how it went, and what they thought of my guy, she wrote back, "Our engineer thinks your guy is a genius." That made me feel great. Wow! Maybe it wasn't such a big mistake hiring him after all.

Over the next couple months, as they're shopping my product at different toy fairs all over the world, we were going back and forth trying to come to terms for the licensing agreement. I really wanted to work with them and tried to make the deal happen, but there was an indemnification section in the contract that Glenn warned me would be dangerous. Basically, they wanted me to indemnify them if I was ever sued for patent infringement. In other words, if anyone sued them or me, it would be all on me to fight it in the courts.

Glenn went on to explain that they could continue to produce and sell the product if I got sued, and they wouldn't be a part of it because I would have indemnified them. On top of that, they would, according to the contract, not pay me during the time of any lawsuit, but they'd still be allowed to continue to make and sell the product. So while I'm tied up in a lawsuit and probably needing money, they would be holding my royalty payments until the lawsuit was over.

In my life I've been caught up in legal dealings. My custody battles alone showed that these things could take years to resolve. Plus if, God forbid, I *lost* the lawsuit, I wouldn't only owe my profit of, let's say, fifty cents a Hair Blinger, I would also owe the two dollars, let's say, per Hair Blinger that *they* had made.

I didn't understand how that made any sense. "How are they my partner?" I asked Glenn. "How are we working together?"

This didn't seem like a partnership to me—with the big guy being free and clear and the little guy, or gal, taking all the risk. Glenn and I believed in the patent claims, but anyone can sue anyone over anything at any time. It could have ruined me financially, fighting in courts with only my Arbonne income to sustain us. It was just too big a risk.

I told the CEO that I was sorry, but I couldn't in good conscience do the deal if the indemnity clause was in it. That it was too risky for me and my family. I was hoping she would remove it from the agreement and we'd do the deal—it was the only stipulation at that point, but she didn't. Instead she simply replied, "Okay, fine. Where do you want me to send the check?"

It was disappointing, but I didn't know what she meant about the check, so I called Glenn. "We're not doing the deal, but why is the CEO talking about a check?"

"I wasn't going to let them take your product to Dallas and test the market without giving you money if they didn't do the deal with you." It had been right there in the eight-paragraph letter of understanding. But that letter was written by my attorney whom I had worked with for over two years at this point and totally trusted. So I just signed it and never read it. I had no idea he'd put that in there.

I was like, "Oh my gosh! Thank you. How much is it for?"

He said, "Ten thousand dollars."

I just got the $10,000 I should have won on *Funderdome*. Thank you, God.

In case I haven't stressed this enough, you need a good attorney, and Glenn is the best.

When we first started working together, I read over what he sent me and I would call him with many questions. About ten minutes into probably the third patent call with him, and me questioning the fifth item of thirty written into one of our filings, I finally said, "You know what, I think I'm just gonna trust you know what you're doing here. I don't need to go over the rest of these, unless you want to?"

He said, "No. I think it's good."

I think he appreciated that, and I'm pretty sure I heard a little sigh of relief. I bet, like engineers, attorneys get tired of non-attorneys questioning their work.

Meanwhile, Firm 4 had come up with a new design concept by mid-October.

Third concept design, Firm 4, October 2017.

But by early November, it had still not been prototyped, so it was clear there was no way we were going to hit Christmas. I asked Jason if he could make up a cute card to mail to all my Kickstarter supporters, with a picture of the new design on it. We even glued a Swarovski crystal on each of them and sent one out to all 131 Kickstarter backers as an apology for missing Christmas.

In December, we also posted a video of the new design so the backers could see that we were still working diligently. We shared our future goals and hopeful deadlines for 2018. I imagined we'd get a "Thanks for the update," but instead, people were starting to get rude and mean on my site. Like I'd let them down and ruined their Christmas. None of my friends, mind you. Just a few of the backers I didn't know. It might as well have been all of them for how it felt though. I'm a huge advocate for the customer and good customer service. I felt sick.

I started seriously disliking my Kickstarter and became filled with anxiety at the thought of even looking at it. Between the haters, Firm 4's shenanigans, and the second school event I was now chairing, I think this is around the time when my eye started twitching. No one understood everything I was doing to make this product happen. The tremendous pressure I felt and sense of failure that was growing daily. I knew they didn't get it, but not commenting or trying to appease them only made their comments increase and get worse. I was living a customer service nightmare. All I care about in business are my customers. But I had nothing new. I was struggling just to get a weekly update myself from my engineer. I was more upset than anyone but didn't think that was a good thing to share. And to pretend everything was all right was not going to work for me either. So I just avoided it all together. Not the best decision.

Then, a few days before Christmas, my engineer finally got the completed prototype back from China. He reviewed it and sent me a video of proposed changes, telling me he was going to have those design changes to China before Christmas, and that they could produce and ship out the second prototype within a week.

I was getting excited again. I thought maybe I could take my product to the New York Toy Fair in February. He thought that was totally possible and said confidently he could have fifteen to twenty working prototypes in packaging by then. So I took a portion of the money I'd just received from the toy company and signed up for the New York Toy Fair. He assured me we would be ready, adding "barring an act of God."

On January 10, 2018, I finally got the first prototype from him. Why it took three weeks to ship I didn't dare question. It had issues, but I couldn't have been more thrilled to hold something real in my hands. Though I didn't like the shape, I was just grateful for a product, and with only six plastic parts.

Working prototype of third design, Firm 4, January 2018.

Unfortunately, it was awkward for an adult to hold, and a child would not have been able to use it because of the width between the handles. It also had a flaw in the design in that it would definitely pinch users' hands, which wasn't good. You also had to remove three separate parts just to open and load it.

The prototype came with display discs, meaning they didn't have any gems on them and were just to show the idea of what the discs might look like, so we weren't able to test if any of it would actually work.

Nonetheless, it had been a long time coming, so I was happy to finally have it.

Unfortunately, my happiness was short-lived. Though design iterations were going to be submitted before Christmas—his deadline, not mine—I found out a week later, the third week of January, that nothing had been submitted yet.

As you may know, China shuts down for practically the whole month of February for their New Year's celebration. So if the revised prototype didn't get shipped to me by February 8, when the factory would be closing, we would be hard-pressed to hit homecoming and prom season in May—a big next target of mine after Christmas. My salon friends were all so excited for this device and had been for a couple years already. I was feeling horrible, thinking not only did I miss Christmas, but now homecoming. I couldn't believe it. What happened to 2017?

And what about him promising me, *barring an act of God*, to have the product ready for the New York Toy Fair at the end of February? Did he just forget? When I stood up to him, which was actually me just suggesting we do the prototyping in America, not China, and to maybe bring in more resources, he blew up. He sent me back this long, in-your-face email about how he'd been offended by my email and told me that:

- My mind has been irrevocably poisoned by my past engineers that let me down
- I wouldn't bring anything substantial to the development process and I really only asked to be more involved because I just didn't believe in him and wanted to monitor him more closely because I'm nervous and afraid
- If I had the skill set to do this myself, then it wouldn't have taken me all these years and developers only to be at square one
- His clients love him and shout his name from the rooftops [I'm not making any of this up] and return to him for new projects over and over

- He knows what he's doing and he's very good at it
- He could hire more people, yes, but my budget doesn't accommodate that
- I can't ask for timeliness, quality, and low cost—I can only have two, which is a hard-and-fast rule of business called the project manager triangle

These were just the highlights; the email went on—and on. At the end, he gave me two options: one was that he'd send me back all the money I paid him, $17,100; or two, that I just trust that he'd make it happen.

I actually struggled with this. *God, Angie, you don't trust anyone. You need to just trust him.* That was what I was hearing in my head, so I started to type up a response with an apology. And just then, I got a phone call.

Over the years this kind of thing had happened a few key times. By this point, I believed that when I got interrupted, with a phone call or something with the kids, it was for a reason. I started paying attention to the timing of things—especially interruptions when I was feeling stressed or anxious. I started seeing sidetracks as course corrections. I stopped and had second thoughts before sending that email. I believed that this was a lesson God really wanted me to learn.

After my phone call, it hit me. This guy is a gambler. He's rolling the dice and banking on my good nature and low confidence at this point that I would take option two. That I should be lucky to have him. He's putting me down and then seemingly saving me. "Just trust me. Here I am, taking you on, for very little money, trying to help you. And look how you're treating me," he'd also said in that email.

I almost fell for it. I think I had at other times when I had been frustrated with him and feeling helpless. But not this time.

I have realized in my life that if you want something to happen on the outside, it may be that the best place to start is on the inside. You want change in your life? Change. Because we can't change others—

no matter how much we try. We only have control over ourselves. I've heard it said that you take yourself with you wherever you go. Are you the reason the same thing keeps happening? What's the common denominator? If you're on your fourth divorce and all your exes just had one marriage (and that was with you)—ding, ding, ding! It might be the call that needs answering is coming from inside your own house.

Was I the problem? I had to face this question before I made another move. No more reacting—I needed more reflecting. He was right about one thing: I had been through numerous engineering firms, it was coming up on four years now, and I still didn't have a Hair Blinger that worked with fewer than ten plastic parts (not that I knew of anyway, since Firm 4 hadn't produced even a video of the device pushing a single gem out). I needed to do some real soul searching. Maybe I had led when I needed to follow. Spoken when I needed to listen. Ran when I needed to walk. Reacted when I needed to pray.

Failure is humbling.

But it also gives you greater appreciation for when things go right. When people do right by you. It gives you better understanding when someone says, "This might take a little longer than I had thought it would," or "We can't do it that way, but here's an option."

Remember, you may just need to *grow* there, not just *get* there. God may need you to get something so that you're ready when it happens. To build you internally to a place where only he knows you'll need to be when the right moment arrives. And that he's got you in his hands, but it's on his timeline.

I wasn't sure what I was going to do with Firm 4 at this point, but I knew whatever I decided, it wasn't going to be decided that day, maybe not even that week. Sometimes doing nothing is doing something. I needed to pray and be still. To listen for *his* voice.

The next day, I called Vishaal Verma with Design Anomaly, previously known as Prospect 2. His firm was the one I had rejected the year before for Firm 3. I didn't call to hire him though. With complete humility in my heart, I called to ask him if he'd evaluate the latest design as well as the email Firm 4 had just sent me about how I didn't understand the design process and was simply jaded from my previous engineering letdowns. I told him I would compensate him for his time and that I just needed his expert opinion.

Vishaal agreed to look at it and help me if he could.

I then called Glenn, who also has an engineering degree (have I mentioned he's brilliant?) and asked for the same candid opinion. I said, "Please don't sugarcoat it." I wanted genuine feedback even if it hurt.

He said he'd be happy to give his assessment.

I sent both of them Firm 4's email, my comments in red, and the engineering files I had up to that point and waited—patiently— probably for the first time in my life.

Then I went back to praying, along with taking a deep introspection of my very being. *Who am I and what am I doing?*

Chapter 15

"Just keep swimming, just keep swimming..."

*~**Dory**, Finding Nemo*

So here we were again, back at the starting line. You may recall a similar opening just a few chapters back (and a few other places in this book). This time though, not only did I not have a working prototype or a working tool, but I was pretty much out of working capital, and I no longer had marketing working for me through a TV show.

What a difference a year can make. Or not.

Nothing changed. Oh, wait, actually it did. But for the worse.

◊ ◊ ◊

"The measure of success is not whether you have a tough problem to deal with, but whether it is the same problem you had last year."

*~**John Foster Dulles**, American diplomat and former United States Secretary of State*

What am I doing wrong?

I think at this point most would ask why didn't I quit or, the more entertaining question, why did I keep going? There is a difference. Quitting is much easier. But to keep going, especially after so much failure, that's way harder.

I can't answer why I kept going. I know I never thought about quitting. I was on a mission from God. The only thing I was questioning was why he chose me. I didn't get that, and the only thing that makes any sense about why I didn't question the rest is that I was filled with the Holy Spirit. I literally had strength and resilience that doesn't make sense now when I look back. I also didn't feel delusional. I felt compelled. I didn't feel let down. I felt I just hadn't gotten it right. I had to figure it out, and until I did that, I was going to keep going. It was that simple.

I do think we hear way too often that life is short, and it may be why people quit when they should stay the course. We don't want to live in pain. I think many people feel like they have to be happy right now because they don't have much time.

Don't fall for that. Life is long. And too long to be complacent. Playing it safe has its own set of risks. Life isn't meant to be this smooth park ride that never makes you sick, slows down, or isn't sometimes a little too rocky. And our happiness is not the end-all, be-all. There are going to be hard times and, really, thank goodness for them.

When I look back on my life, I can see that it was the toughest times that gave me the most personal growth, that deepened my humanity, strengthened my relationships, and revealed my utter dependence on God in my life. Those were the times that molded me into the person I am today.

My publisher, Arthur Klebanoff, recently said to me, "You seem to be a genius at whimsy." I loved that. I had never been described that way before, and yet, I know that probably comes from pain somewhere along my life. I don't mean that in a bad way, but more in a badge-of-honor way. Self-development pain. Gotta love it. Maybe the product I was really developing on this journey was me.

"Consider it pure joy, my brothers and sisters, whenever you face trials of many kinds, because you know that the testing of your faith produces perseverance."

~James 1:2–3

Let life be all it is. Embrace *every* part. The bad may be changing you for the good.

> *"More than that, we can rejoice when we run into problems and trials, for we know that they help us develop endurance. And endurance develops strength of character. And character strengthens our confident hope of salvation. And this hope will not lead to disappointment. For we know how dearly God loves us, because he has given us the Holy Spirit which fills our hearts with His love."*
>
> ~**Romans** 5:3–5

Make it more important to do something right and finish a job, than being happy and never shedding a tear. Happiness is just a feeling, a temporary state of mind. Find joy in the work, in your purpose.

> *"Let perseverance finish the work He started in you so that you may be complete and not lacking anything."*
>
> ~**James** 1:4

Take quitting off the table.

Vishaal got back to me that same day I sent everything to him and confirmed that Firm 4 knew what he was doing for the most part, but that his design was lacking aesthetically. He thought Firm 3's design was much more attractive (the hairbrush design), and I had to agree. I explained to him why I terminated our contract with Firm 3—that they missed deadlines, that they didn't provide a true working prototype, and the biggest, that they didn't keep it to under ten plastic parts. That they were hostile and malicious. (I didn't really share that part.) I told him that their product design had twenty-two plastic parts, even more than the previous design, which had eighteen. He asked for their design files. Once he looked at Firm 3's engineering files, he confirmed that he found their design "insanely complex," and told me even he was having trouble following what was happening inside their device.

I felt vindicated. Though my choices in selecting the engineering firms had *clearly* been wrong to this point, my decision to let them go was spot-on. I hired Vishaal later that week, and he accepted me as a client, battered and bruised as I was.

I was finally ready to reply to Firm 4's email. I wrote, "Thank you very much for your time. I'll take option one, please."

I only got half of the money back and it came months later, but it allowed me to make my second payment of three to Vishaal. By the grace of God I was still alive, and Hair Blinger was still a possibility.

Vishaal picked up my job on February 7, at essentially ground zero. When he told me it would be at least six to eight months just to get to a fully functioning prototype (precisely what he had said the year before, and I didn't hire him because I couldn't wait that long) and that it would be $10,000 more than what he proposed the year before, I didn't bat an eye. I was done trying to make things happen the way I thought they should. I truly, and finally, turned it all over to him. (God, not Vishaal. Well, a little part to Vishaal.)

Because of my short association with the toy company, I knew I had to book a booth at Dallas Toy Fair in order to get Hair Blinger on the shelves the following Christmas. Vishaal had told me it was going to be possibly eight months before we'd have a working prototype, so I went ahead and booked my booth right then. The Toy Association let me roll my New York Toy Fair deposit into the show in Dallas. Dallas Toy Fair was the first week of October, eight months was the end of September, so worst case, I'd show up with one working prototype. I could make that work. If he made it happen by then, I was going to be there.

It's important to have goals, but deadlines are how goals happen, at least for me. The toy show was the deadline that made perfect sense. It's also why I had Christmas and homecoming as goals. Just another great business lesson I had learned from Arbonne. Every month we'd work our businesses, but it was the last week of the month that our numbers would double from what they had been midmonth and then the last day, many times, they'd double again. I learned from this that if we had a year to make a goal happen, most of us would only do a quarter of it in the first six months, half by Christmas, and the rest in the last week. It's human nature, I guess.

But an amazing thing happened when I finally *let go and let God*. By March 9, only thirty days after starting, Vishaal had not only one concept designed for Hair Blinger, but two, each with ten or fewer plastic parts.

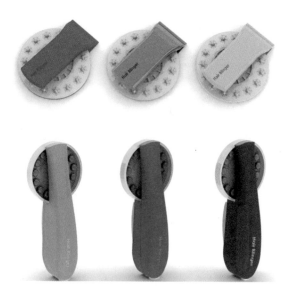

Concept design of fourth and fifth designs, Firm 5, Design Anomaly, March 9, 2018. Two design concepts engineered within thirty days of hiring Vishaal!

By March 21, twelve days later and just forty-two days after starting, Vishaal, my fifth engineer, sent me pictures and a video from his office in Chicago of the two prototypes assembled and fully functioning.

They were in my hands by March 26. He said, "I made two so that you could choose which one you liked better."

Well hello, Vishaal. Seven weeks earlier I had practically nothing, was completely discouraged, and still at square one, and now, I had two working prototypes in my hands. *Options! What a wonderful turn of events.*

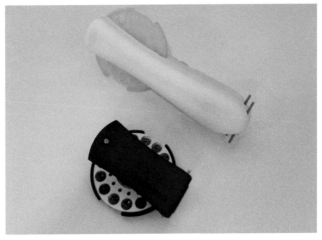

Working prototypes of fourth and fifth designs, Firm 5, Design Anomaly, March 21, 2018. Two functioning prototypes in my hands within forty-seven days of hiring Vishaal!

I knew right away which one I loved and if you know the product, you do too! It had two fewer parts than the other one, which was of course why I chose it.

It was amazing. And for the first time, the development side was fun.

After that, we fiddled around with different ideas and improvements, increasing the spacing for where the hair went, making the pegs a bit higher where the disc went so it would stay in place better, adding a cover to the disc area, possible ways to lock the device, different ways we could get the handle out of the way for certain hair styles, etc. We made several more prototypes until we had everything just the way we wanted it. It was finally the product I had dreamed of making years before.

One of the prototypes he made had an actual lock on it, but it was another part. I said, "No. No more parts!" I was like the Soup Nazi on *Seinfeld*. "No more parts for you, Hair Blinger!" So instead, he came up with this little rubber band lock—just a cute way to keep it closed. It was perfect. The whole experience was actually enjoyable. Who knew?

Vishaal knew he was my fifth engineer. And I also let him know that I didn't have all the money yet for his contract when I first hired him, but that I would find a way to make sure he was paid. He trusted me. And I trusted God to make that happen. I think Vishaal was one of the first engineers who truly listened to me too—and he probably felt a little sorry for me. I also didn't try to dictate how it was all going to go with him or push him in any way—more because of weariness than wisdom. I got out of the way, and trusted God to deliver—finally.

Vishaal was all about the prototypes. He sent me a video link about the importance of making several of them. He made many Hair Blinger prototypes and was shocked that the firm I'd hired over him the year before only made two before trying to shuffle me off to the manufacturer.

I also learned from Vishaal that it's about six to ten times more expensive to manufacture here than in China. It's hard to compete with Chinese pricing. Even with any mistakes, shipping costs, and time to get it from there to here (five weeks on a boat), you still can't beat their pricing. If it were made in America, Hair Blinger would need to retail for $150, not $20. Wages are just a lot less in China. Americans are paid more. That's what it mostly boils down to. At those prices, I would have had so many competitors, even Chinese companies, copying my product and undercutting me, with or without my patent. Unethical companies don't care about the patent with a small company like mine. They work those kinds of lawsuits into their margins.

Most start-ups can't afford to pay a million-plus dollars to defend their patent anyway. Business insurance may be able to cover you to fight anyone who infringes on your patent, but you still end up losing money—and the operation who stole your idea can still make millions while they fight you in court if it's a hot product.

Vishaal's product design was something that could not only do the job but would make the product affordable in the market if produced in China.

At the time, we were living in Pennsylvania, but the kids were going to a school in Delaware. This was possible because my ex was still in Delaware, so they were still zoned for the schools there. The problem was that our commute was horrible, and when Cambria was accepted to the high school that spring, I realized it was going to be another six to seven years of us making this commute, with Christian in middle school and Evan coming up on sixth grade.

From 2014 to 2018, we'd leave at six thirty every morning—all of us, including Grace, who was only two months old when we moved to Pennsylvania. We'd drive forty minutes to Wilmington to drop off Cambria, then Christian, Evan, Grace, and I went to a coffeehouse, The Well, near Christian's and Evan's elementary school, where we'd hang out for an hour before dropping them off. Grace and I wouldn't be back home until about nine thirty a.m.; then we'd reverse it in the afternoon, driving back and picking everyone up at two p.m. and then not getting home until four thirty p.m. I was literally commuting about five hours each day—and I worked from home!

I had no problem with it for years, because we loved our home. It was like a dream that I had this beautiful, spacious home as a single mom. I felt blessed. I still managed to find time to work on my Hair Blinger and Arbonne businesses—I made all my phone calls on the commutes and only did computer work at home. I had snacks and drinks in the car, along with trash cans, paper towels, wet wipes, tissues, pencils, pens, sharpies, scissors, envelopes (for school forms)—anything and everything I would possibly need for the kids was in the car.

We were managing, except when someone forgot a book bag or their coat or a permission form. Going back threw everything out of whack. All the driving was slowly getting to me, and I was starting to exhibit feelings of rage against other drivers on the road, which wasn't good for anyone to witness, especially my children.

I was secretly starting to think how much better our lives could be without the commute, imagining myself in bunny slippers, sipping my tea calmly at the kitchen island, shooing my beautiful children out the front door to catch the bus after feeding them a nutritious, home-cooked breakfast. Then I'd come out of my stupor and start cursing at the driver who'd just cut me off.

The kids loved our house. They weren't complaining about the commute. I knew as soon as I started complaining, they'd all go negative, so I kept it to myself, thinking, "I have to get this figured out. I can't do this anymore." Leaving the schools wasn't an option. I knew we had to move back to Delaware.

A week after Cambria's acceptance, I became adamant about selling my dream home and buying a new house in Delaware by summer. I had to let the kids in on my plan so they'd have plenty of time to process. And so they'd stop questioning me every time I drove particularly slowly through a random neighborhood for no apparent reason. As suspected, they all started crying when I told them what I felt needed to happen for our family, but within a week, after enduring the commute for so long and realizing they wouldn't have to do it anymore, they all got excited about moving back to Delaware and riding the bus to school. We were the most negative bunch of commuters that route has ever had. We were all so bitter in the car now. The kids were even flipping people off—kidding!

By May, we were still looking for a house. It was tough. The cost of living was so different in Delaware. There was no way we could afford something comparable to what we had.

Around this time, I learned that Vishaal had a contact in China, something he didn't have when we'd started. He'd also delivered the fourth or fifth prototype of his darling design, so at this point, we were ready for the next step—manufacturing. And that's when it hit me: I've got a working prototype, I'll have cash from selling my house, and now there's a Chinese manufacturing contact.

I knew the next step after we had a good prototype was manufacturing, and I thought I was going to have to get an investor, but so far no one was interested in investing in my product. No one saw it like I did. (And there was no way I was going to do another crowd fund with many of my Kickstarter backers telling me how much they despised me on a regular basis.) I thought, why not invest the money from the sale of my house into Hair Blinger, instead of buying a new home? We could rent an apartment for a year or two until it was successful enough. I was very excited at the thought of this.

I had to make sure my kids were on board though. An apartment would be too big of a shock for them compared to what we had. So I got them together and asked, "What would you think if I took the money from the sale of our home and put it into the Hair Blinger?" My eyes were wide with excitement. "I can take the money from the house and use it to build the tool in China. Instead of buying a new home, we'll just rent an apartment for a year or so. What do you think?"

At first, they all looked at me like I had asked this question in French and not English. Then Cambria said, "You've got to do it, Mom."

And I was like, "All right!" I was so excited to have their buy-in, but I don't think any of them really understood what I had just asked of them. I think if they had, they would have all started crying again. My poor children. I can't tell you how grateful I am that this all worked out in the end.

Right away, I switched from looking for homes for sale and started looking for rentals. There was nothing. I scrolled the sites every day for a week or so until a townhome came on the market only a block from where we used to live in Delaware. There was literally nothing else in the school district for rent.

When I picked the kids up from school, we went to look at it. My kids are better rule followers than me. This is a good thing, but it makes it hard for me to be normal around them. I feel like I'm going to freak them out at any moment by doing something prohibited or frowned upon, like double parking outside the grocery store. They hate when I do that.

We were sitting in the car outside the teeny-tiny house, just looking at it, when one of them said, "Let's go knock on the door and ask to see inside."

Knowing this was not the proper way and that they wouldn't want to do it the wrong way, I explained that I had already emailed (and called) the agent, and that we needed to wait for them to respond. "But why can't we just knock on the door?" they asked again. I went on to clarify that people don't like to be bothered—that's why they hire Realtors and property managers. Completely out of character, my three oldest (Grace was only four, so she was just sitting there, probably oblivious) started begging for me to knock. I reluctantly agreed, confused at the total role reversal, and we headed to the front door. The owner, Jesse, answered and graciously let us in, saying, "Wow, that was fast. The rental just went online today."

I said, "I know," and after only a few minutes of checking it out I said, "Don't let anyone else rent this place. I'm your renter." I can be pretty assertive when it comes to housing for my children, and we basically rented it on the spot.

I sold my home, making $115,000 in cash, and I also sold half of our belongings since we were going from five thousand square feet to two thousand. The money went toward making the remaining payments for my booth, filming videos to show there, flying Jason out to shoot the videos and take the photos needed, marketing, and packaging. And of course, there was the tooling, which was now only $24,000 (from more than $80,000, if you remember), because there were only eight plastic parts. Yay! Then, hopefully, we'd have money left from all that to produce a small product run that I could use to demo in Dallas, fulfill my Kickstarter, and make some sales from my website.

Moving that summer was a nightmare. I did it on my own and didn't hire movers because I wanted to preserve capital. I had to order six of those moving pods in all, delivered one at a time to my old home, filled, and then dropped off and unloaded at my townhome. After my second pod arrived to be filled, for some reason, my friends stopped answering my calls or texts. I managed though.

Once we moved in, the air conditioner broke, and for six weeks the property manager wouldn't come out and fix it. They said it was because I was moving, and the doors being opened so much, and that it was an extra-hot summer. These were the reasons I was given about why it "seemed" like the AC wasn't working. I bought Target out of all their fans.

"Oh God, please give me assurances that what I'm doing is right," I would pray as we sweated our butts off that summer, and I'd thank him in advance for making it all work out as he promised.

"And we know that all things work together for good to them that love God, to them who are the called according to his purpose" (Romans 8:28).

I believed, thought, spoke, and prayed this way. I refused to complain.

We built the tool over the summer. There's a twelve-hour difference between here and China. They're sleeping when we're awake, so many of the calls happened after the kids were in bed.

I loved working with China. Janice, my main contact at the factory and who headed the group, was great, and she and I were an amazing team. I'm detail-oriented, and so is she. She'd catch things I missed, and I'd catch things she missed. And thank goodness we were both this way, because Hair Blinger has a lot of details—size, color, and shape of rhinestones, plus quantities, then double all those details for the Swarovski crystal packages. Then you have to roll that out with the packaging, the wording, bar codes, and shipping labels, and everything has to sync up and match up. Then there's the pricing, shipping, FOBs, fulfillment. You should see the spreadsheets I have of just creating SKUs with matching GS1 codes (the codes you need in order to have bar codes on your packaging—a whole international thing with every company in the world).

Speaking of spreadsheets, one of the best moves I made in the summer of 2018 was to create an Excel document that I sent my manufacturer with my top four goals for the year. This detailed for Janice when I needed to hit certain business objectives and *why* they were important to me. It listed all the small targets we hoped and needed to hit that year, besides our big goal of five thousand devices and ten thousand refill packs by the end of the year and it included intermediary goals, such as having thirty production units for Dallas Toy Fair in October and three hundred devices for our Kickstarter supporters by the end of November.

Sharing my goals helped Janice understand other important business objectives I had and to help make them happen if she could. It also helped me to know early on what they could commit to doing and what they couldn't. It eliminated a lot of assumptions on both sides. If I hadn't shared that with her when I did, we would not have had product in time for Dallas Toy Fair.

Communicating your goals with your team early and often is big. I know for me when I understand the value of something, I get behind it more, I push a little harder, and I feel the importance of the work I'm doing. So I had a column just for why it was important to the company (and the manufacturer) to hit that goal. Let your team in on your vision and the big picture. Otherwise, the greater things might get swallowed up by the smaller day-to-day items.

That summer I knew I needed to put a team together to help me get ready for the show. I couldn't do all these next steps on my own.

I hired Kimberly "Kimmie" Anderson in August. She was cleaning houses at the time, and though she also had a full-time job, she seemed unhappy and ready for a change. Plus, I thought she was such an amazing young lady, and I saw her doing much greater things. She's so sharp and talented, and with a heart of gold. In the two years I worked with her every day Monday through Friday, I don't think I ever saw her not in good spirits or without a smile on her face. She's one of my dearest friends and a bright light for not only me but my children.

I hired her to be head of fulfillment. She didn't know anything about fulfillment of a product, but I knew she would figure out exactly how it needed to happen, how it worked, and what it would take to move Hair Blingers from a factory in China to a customer or retailer in the USA. And if you think that's an easy gig, you don't know anything about fulfillment.

I called Jason too. I needed him and felt he was the best at what he did. We hadn't spoken in a few months, and at first I didn't feel he was that interested. I didn't blame him though. I had gone through three designs and two engineering firms, and was on my third in the one year he'd known me. I'm sure that wasn't reaffirming. But I knew this device was it and we were finally ready for next steps, so I pursued him. We started talking about what I needed for my booth, website, and packaging. We already had the logo and some good images from the year before, but nothing with the new product.

In August I flew him out to Delaware to do the photography for the packaging and website and to create videos to play in the booth at the toy fair. This was a much better experience for both of us. Not only was I not trying to coordinate a three-day shoot in another state from a packed RV on a road trip, I had resources, connections from my own town, money to pay the stylists and makeup people—not trying to barter these costs down like before—but mostly, not being on vacation, I had focused time to do all this planning.

It was a very exciting and nerve-racking summer, but mostly I had this feeling of "This is finally happening and it's gonna be great!"

Photo shoot. Summer 2018. Cambria and Grace up top!
Look how Cambria has grown since day one.

Chapter 16

"A gem cannot be polished without friction, nor a man perfected without trials."

> ~**Lucius Annaeus Seneca**, Hispanic-Roman Philosopher

A couple of weeks before Dallas Toy Fair, I was working in my office (the couch in my living room) with Kimmie, who was in her office (my kitchen island). I called out to her, "There's something that happens the night before the show. That Monday." I was sure of this because of what Firm 4 had told me the year before when he'd met with the toy company's engineer—that they knew Walmart wanted Hair Blinger before the show had even started.

Kimmie quickly started clicking away on the keys on her computer and then shouted back, "You're right! There's a Women in Toys event the day before the show. Walmart is there, and *you've* got to be there."

I immediately jumped on to their website, but when I went in to sign up, I saw that registration had already closed. "Aw, we missed the deadline."

Kimmie said, "Sign up anyway!"

I was already on it and yelled back, "Don't worry. I am."

When I looked over the pages for the Women in Toys Empowerment Day, as I learned it was called, I saw not only Walmart, but all these toy companies were going to be there to hear pitches as well. This made sense for the event and other toy inventors, but not for me. I wasn't going to license my product because I didn't need to anymore. I was going to manufacture it myself, self-produce as they call it. I had a tool, a budding team, and now I just needed sales. I only wanted to get my product in front of Walmart. But I decided to schedule two pitch sessions with a couple of the toy companies that morning as warm-up practice for my Walmart pitch at noon.

What I would come to learn was that Women in Toys (WIT) is a wonderful nonprofit group that helps women get their toy ideas into the world. Inventors and creators can pitch their product to different toy companies the day before Dallas Toy Fair each year, and you don't need to have a prototype to attend. You also don't have to have a booth, like I did, to go. Anyone is welcome to go that day before the show and share their idea, gather feedback, and maybe even get some interest in their product from the toy companies, but also, from Walmart. I was so excited that they accepted my late registration, but I had no idea just how significant and empowering their empowerment day was going to be.

I arrived at the World Trade Center in Dallas on Thursday, several days before the show, which started on Tuesday, and the WIT Empowerment Day was on Monday. I was the only one setting up my booth that whole weekend. Each day I kept thinking people would be there the next day, only to be the only one again. I eventually realized everyone else probably had a team of people to assemble their booths. I was right. Everyone else showed up Monday and put their entire booths together in one day. I was so thankful I didn't know this, or I might have shown up Saturday night thinking I could do it in one day too, and would have been exhausted or extremely stressed for Monday's empowerment day. Being alone there for the whole weekend worked to my advantage. It allowed me the space and time to make our booth shine that much more.

I really didn't know if anyone would even like my product before I got to Dallas, but for some reason I felt like something big was about to happen. I had this crazy sense of it. Nothing specific, just a feeling, really. I was filled with anticipation. There was this energy all around, and inside me, and I felt like I was glowing. I don't know how else to describe it. I just felt my moment was about to arrive, even though I had nothing concrete to back that feeling up.

First day in Dallas World Trade Center, September 27, 2018.

I had hired a consultant that summer, my friend and former neighbor Manda Koss, to help with the overall company direction and marketing. She was inspired by a "Rock Your Hair" campaign at CosmoProf and wanted our booth to have that same feel, including a step-and-repeat banner that people could take photos in front of and post on Instagram and other social media sites.

Jason created the banner with bokeh accents, basically a cool blurring effect, that made it pop. He designed and sized it with Kimmie's help to cover one whole wall of our booth. It was so beautiful and professional-looking.

By the second day, the union guys and I started to become friends. A couple of them even started to offer to help me hang things.

You know, a lot of amazing and powerful things can come from just being nice to people—never thinking you're better than someone else. It's easy to think you're above others when you've had some advantages in your life, like if your parents have money, or you're naturally beautiful. But like I tell my children, it's not about looks or money as much as we're taught to believe by society. Those can come and go and often will. It's about your heart. That love toward others and having a grateful heart, the unseen possessions, are much more valuable. They trump everything else. I encourage them to just be kind, even to people you're upset with. Pray for them especially. In doing so, you will cultivate all the most important riches in the world—those of the heart.

On Friday, Jason drove down from Oklahoma, bringing our high-top white table and two leather-back chairs Kimmie had ordered and had shipped to his house (to save on docking fees), along with some cool lights he had. I covered the plastic convention booth chairs and table they supplied in white fabric. I brought some white accent rugs and even included a bit of my own bookshelf decor from home—a carved wood sign that said *Dream*. When it was done, I thought our booth looked darling. It ended up having a fun, upscale look, and I loved our little high-top seating area to bling hair. I felt we looked professional, like we knew what we were doing and not like the rookies we actually were.

We had fun posters made featuring Cambria and some of her best girlfriends as models. I liked how some of the posters could be read two ways too: either *be* Bold, *be* Focused, *be* First, *be* Sassy, and so on, or just Bold, Focused, First, Sassy.

That Saturday, only two days before I was to present to Walmart at the Women in Toys event, my product arrived from China to my hotel in Dallas. I hugged that FedEx guy! I brought all the boxes to my room and spread everything out all over the bed. My product in packaging! It was like a real product. All my hard work that summer, mostly done in the middle of the night, was there right in front of me. Heck, all my hard work from the last four years—laid out on the bed. It was beautiful!

My product produced and in packaging—amazing thing to finally see!

Later that day, I was at the Starbucks in the World Trade Center when two women noticed the bling in my hair. "I like your sparkles," one of them told me.

I had some of the packaged Hair Blingers in my bag, and I was more than eager to show them off. I excitedly pulled a couple of them out. They both bought one, for forty dollars each. They didn't even balk at the price. I made eighty dollars the very first day I had product in the US! I still have those four twenty-dollar bills. I plan to frame them someday, one for each of my children, maybe with a little motivational poem I'll write about never giving up on their dreams.

My friends Patrice and Shelley arrived on Sunday. Shelley, who runs Chalk Me Up T-shirts, also registered late because she heard about it from me, and she managed to get some meetings booked with the toy companies too. Patrice came to help me pitch Walmart and run the booth. They didn't seem to mind staying in this hole-in-the-wall hotel room I had booked to save money. We knew we only needed it for sleeping and showering—we were working girls on a mission. "Next year we'll stay at the Renaissance!" I told them.

Patrice had helped me with the school events I had chaired in 2017 and 2018. We knew we liked each other and worked well together. Over the course of the weekend, she told me she was feeling like she was being touched. Like she was being called. She knew about my faith because I had openly shared it with her many times. Plus, she was seeing firsthand this dream unfolding, a dream she knew I believed came from God.

Before getting to work, Patrice, Shelley, and I headed to Target to try to find some cute pillows for the chairs in the booth. When we pulled into the parking spot, I said, "I just need to get three pillows that say something like 'Sparkle' on them." We headed into the store, and within minutes, we found exactly three pillows with the word *Sparkle* on them.

"Yep, that's right!" I said as I grabbed all my pillows and headed to the register with pride.

Patrice converted right then!

It wasn't a surprise to me, finding those pillows like we did and so quickly. It says in the Bible, "You have not because you ask not" (James 4:2). And Joel Osteen has said many times that you have to speak your words out loud for what you want to see happen in your life. (And also why you need to be careful about what you speak out loud.)

I knew my time had come. I felt it in my heart, so I wasn't astounded. I knew even bigger things were about to happen. But, that I might have just made a friend a believer—there is no bigger thing than that.

 **DAY 1,429**

The next morning, October 1, 2018, we were getting breakfast inside the area where the WIT event was happening, and I ran into Latitia, a woman I had met while filming *Funderdome* in 2016. She told me she got a licensing deal from this event the year before and asked me, "So you're here to license your product?"

"No. I'm not licensing my product," I told her. "I'm just here to pitch Walmart."

I'd been down that licensing path twice already, and it hadn't worked out. Now I had a working tool that could manufacture millions of Hair Blingers. I was going to be the toy manufacturer. I felt I was seconds away from being in massive business.

I'd already been told by my friend Shelley and others that it was no easy task to get a product on the shelves with retailers if you weren't established. And then, if you missed one delivery or made any mistake with their order, you could be done. Other than that, I didn't get the enormity of what I was intending to do.

To give you an idea, you've got to have millions of dollars to produce the amount of product that a store like Walmart would need. Remember what the founder of the toy company the year before had said: not only did the product have to be on shelves and online, but there also needed to be big advertising on TV and social media—huge marketing campaigns to get the product off the shelves and into the consumers' hands. If you're not marketing that product, and I mean with a big budget, it doesn't matter if it's a fabulous product. If no one knows about it, no one's going to buy it. And if you don't sell, retailers won't reorder. And then it's done.

I believed then, and I still do, that it is possible to do it on your own. It's just extremely difficult, especially if you don't have a good budget, backer, or banker. (Does anyone have a good banker nowadays? I only added it because it started with a *b*!)

At this point, my money was close to being gone. I think I must have a stomach made of steel or something. I mean, I had just hired Kimmie and I wouldn't have the money to pay her come mid-

November. And, probably not the smartest move on my part, I hired her when she was seven months pregnant.

I have operated my business many times from my heart, not my head. When I look back, I think being at this point is what scares me the most about my journey. I had people counting on me now, our house was gone, and I was on the last of my money and in huge debt. And I had people waiting for their product from my Kickstarter the year before who were not happy. But I wasn't feeling scared at all—just the opposite, in fact. I had no clue how precarious the situation was at the time. I could have seen it, but I was blinded to it for some reason. (I know the reason.) I was so confident, and that could only have come from something outside myself.

That morning, during one of the day's first panels, I ended up sitting next to Anne Marie Kehoe, vice president of toys at Walmart, which blew my mind, because she's literally the biggest toy buyer in the world. I'd say that destiny or God had a hand in me sitting at the table next to hers, but really it was because I got the room layout confused and sat in the wrong place. I had my chair facing the side of the room and had to turn around when the panelists started talking to my left!

When I say anyone can be an inventor, I'm really not kidding.

At one point, I noticed out of the corner of my eye that Anne Marie was looking at my badge. I was like, *Oh my gosh, Anne Marie Kehoe just looked at my badge.* My mind started racing. I thought, *Maybe she saw the bling in my hair and wanted to know who I am so she can get it in all her stores?* I knew it had to be something like that. I'm sure it had nothing to do with me facing the wrong way when the speakers started. Ha-ha!

One of the speakers on the panel was Michael Rinzler, from Wicked Cool Toys (WCT). Also speaking were representatives from Hasbro, Basic Fun, and Spinmaster—basically the hottest toy companies in the world. They *are* the toy market. They build the brands and the toys we all have come to love.

After the panel, it was time for our first pitch session with Lisa Wuennemann from PlayMonster. Peg Brom, who handles all things administrative with WIT and is a beautiful person inside and out, escorted Patrice and me into one of the curtained-off rooms. I liked that the rooms were private. There was a round table in each one with four chairs, and Lisa was sitting at the table waiting for us.

She was very nice, and before we'd really even finished our pitch, she started saying things to us that I wasn't quite comprehending. Words like "advance," "5 percent of net sales," and "guarantee on back end." She also said that our price needed to be twenty dollars, not forty dollars as we had suggested.

I just looked at her and wrote it all down, having no idea how to respond. But Patrice, being much quicker on the draw than me, said "A dollar?" like she was disgusted. That's when it clicked: we'd just been made an offer.

Well, that seemed positive and weirdly easy, I thought. She talked to us about next steps and when we needed to get back to her by. We told her she was our first pitch, but that we'd get back to her, thanked her, and left the room. Patrice and I just stared at each other as we walked out.

Peg asked, "How did it go?"

"She just made us an offer," I replied.

Peg glanced up from her clipboard looking surprised. "Oh. Well, that's great. Congratulations!"

"Thank you," I said, still not 100 percent clear about what had really just happened. Patrice and I headed into the hallway to talk in private.

"So I'm thinking we're going to have a great pitch with Walmart," I said cautiously.

"Yeah," she said.

I hated to be critical during all this excitement, but I didn't want her to talk about the money again in case we got another offer. To communicate that, I used the sandwich method: deliver the criticism (the meat) in between two positives (the bread). The critique is easier to swallow this way.

"Okay, so you were so quick in there," I began. "You picked up how much we were getting offered, minutes before me." (The bread.)

Then I added, "Just don't say anything about the money when they make the offer. We can always get it higher later when we enter into actual agreement discussions with my attorney." (The meat.)

Then I closed with, "That's your strong suit besides. You'll help me to close the deal later. We'll talk privately afterward and figure out our next move." (The bread.)

What I was saying about not talking about money reminded me of the old Kenny Rogers song "The Gambler"—you know, about not counting your money while you're sitting at the Women in Toys table. Classic business advice.

The best part of the WIT event for me was the mentoring sessions. These feature tables with one or two women each sitting at them, with a small sign in front explaining what they had expertise in: marketing, merchandising, fulfillment, manufacturing, licensing, and other areas. You get fifteen minutes at each table. By the end of the day, after spending most of it at those tables, Patrice and I felt like we'd earned our MBA in toys in one day. These women were phenomenal. They just shared. They were like, "No, don't do that. Do this!" We couldn't write fast enough. They were so candid and clearly just wanted to help others become successful. These sessions gave us a much better grasp on things.

One of the tables we visited had Lindsey Berger, director of sales for License 2 Play, and Stefanie Barone, VP of design at Wicked Cool Toys.

I instantly wanted to be Stefanie's best friend. She was just cool. I loved her style, her mannerisms, her *je ne sais quoi* (that's French, kids, for "I don't know what"). If this was a scene in a movie, there would have been little floating hearts all around my head as I sat and listened to her talk.

And she loved my product. "I want this for me!" she said.

I loved her even more.

I whispered that I had some I could sell her privately out of my booth the next day. (I didn't know if we were actually allowed to sell products from our booth or not. I felt like I was setting up a fake handbag sale out of the trunk of my car.)

"Great! What booth are you in?" she asked.

I couldn't remember (I had only spent the whole weekend there, duh!) so I asked her for her card. When she gave it to me, I said, "Oh, our next pitch is with your company."

"Wicked Cool Toys?" she asked. We nodded. "Great! I'll walk you in."

As we entered the booth, Stefanie told the cofounder and co-president, Michael Rinzler, whom I'd listened to speak earlier that morning, "You need to see this product. We need this product."

Smiling but clearly concerned, he replied, "Man, Stef, you're putting a lot of pressure on me. She's standing right here. What if I don't like the item?"

Unfazed, she persisted. "Michael, trust me. You're going to love the item."

At that, she left, and Patrice and I started our demo. Within a few minutes, he picked up his phone and held up his hand. "Hold on, I gotta call Jeremy," he said to us. Then, into the phone, he said, "You gotta come down here."

There was silence.

"The seventh floor. The WIT event. No, come down here now. These two ladies just pitched me this product—you need to see it."

Silence.

"Yes, they're sitting right in front of me, but no, there's no pressure. Trust me, you're gonna love it. Just get down here," he said and then hung up.

Have you ever met someone you just knew right away was awesome? That's Michael Rinzler. Imagine more hearts, and maybe stars this time, floating around my head while I talked to him. He was funny, sincere, and not stuffy. And he too, totally loved the product.

A few minutes later, Jeremy showed up, and my life was complete. I had met three amazing individuals in the period of half an hour.

Jeremy is adorable. He has this infectious smile and a heart of gold—and the instant we demoed Hair Blinger for him, he got it. "Can it bling other things?" he asked.

"Sure!" I said. "But we feel the unique value is with hair."

"No," he said. "You've got to show all it can do. And you gotta change the name. It should just be Blinger! Blinger is perfect." With that, he started blinging the whole pitch room. The curtains, the chairs, the table. He was like a little kid with a new toy.

In the pitch room with the founders of WCT,
Michael and Jeremy.

Michael sat back and asked to hear more about my story. He asked me questions like, "How did you come up with this?" I was getting nervous. I hadn't rehearsed anything beyond the pitch, but I tried to answer his questions as calmly as possible. I told him it came to me in a dream—but just the first one, not the second one. I didn't want anyone freaking out about me and God just yet.

I told him about selling my home and using the money to build the tool in China. That even though I was a single mom, how I just believed in the idea so much.

He was surprised to learn that I'd already tooled it. Then he told me, "Go home. Pack up your booth. You found your partners."

I was like, "We just got here! You're our second pitch and the first one made us an offer too."

I didn't have the heart at that moment to tell him I only booked a pitch with them for practice for Walmart. I started to feel bad. I did say, "We're pitching to Walmart next, so we're not stopping here. And I can't close my booth. My team would kill me."

He said he understood and that he'd talk to me more later.

It was hard to say no to Michael. He and Jeremy were awesome and they clearly fit the role as leaders of a toy company—totally fun! But I wasn't intending to say yes to them. I had come here to sell my product to Walmart, and that's what I was determined to do.

Chapter 17

"It's very easy to get a break. It's very hard to be good enough."

~Jerry Seinfeld

After our first two successful pitches, we couldn't wait to talk to Walmart, my dream retailer. My goal.

Patrice and I were still nervous, but we were over-the-top with energy and excitement now too. We had already received two offers for licensing the product. We were confident we could get Walmart on board with Hair Blinger.

Anne Marie Kehoe was VP of toys, but Lisa Bowman, senior toy buyer, is the one who decides which toys get on the shelves. We didn't meet with Anne Marie or Lisa though. When we entered the room, two other buyers, Brandon, who decides which toys Lisa sees in my category, and another toy buyer in a different space, Nate, greeted us. They were both so nice and nonthreatening.

After our demo, Nate asked, "Have you sold this anywhere?"

I legitimately answered him in all sincerity. "Yes! I just sold two on Saturday at the Starbucks! I made eighty dollars!"

If he hadn't given me the smile he gave me at that moment, I might have pulled out the four twenties just to show him. But that smile told me that I had not quite understood the question. It was the kind of smile you'd give a puppy tripping over its own tail. Nevertheless, when we were done, Brandon said he'd bring Lisa by my booth the following day.

After our Walmart pitch, we thought we'd try to get Hair Blinger in front of a couple more toy companies. We saw Jazwares at two p.m. The rep we met with was sweet, but she didn't think Hair Blinger was a fit for their company. God works in mysterious ways though— about a year later, Jazwares would actually be factoring in pretty big for us. But for now, it was a pass.

Spinmaster agreed to see us at five fifteen p.m., at the very end of the day. Just before that meeting, Mary Kay Russell, the executive director of Women in Toys, came up to me and asked, "Would you bling my hair?"

"Sure!" I knew who she was, and I was so touched that she asked me.

As I blinged her hair, I noticed two other women watching. I wasn't sure if they wanted me to bling their hair or if they were just curious. I was thinking it would be rude not to ask them if they wanted to have their hair blinged, but I didn't want to be so presumptuous either. I decided being polite was the right choice.

As I've mentioned, being kind is something I preach about to my kids all the time. It's just so important in life and business. The other thing I teach them is to not worry so much about what others think. It seems contradictory, but it isn't. I'd rather be embarrassed for a few seconds (not worrying what others think) than to seem unkind by ignoring them (be kind), so I asked, "Would y'all like to get your hair blinged too?"

They both replied, "Would you?"

With those two little words, I knew, truly for the first time, I had a product people would like. They could have replied, "No, thanks" or "That's okay," even if they really wanted me to do it. We women do that all the time. We don't seem to want to put anyone out or be seen as pushy. That they responded like that said so much to me.

Within a few moments of Mary Kay and the other two getting blinged, a crowd of women had formed around us, all waiting to get their hair blinged. I broke into my refill packs and started asking what color stone they would like or recommending one based on what they were wearing or their hair color. I was saying things like, "Oh, I think this would be a pretty color for you!"

Women gathering around to get their hair blinged at the
Women in Toys event.

As I was blinging, I started to notice that maybe because of the pampering, or even just the shimmer they could see they were getting, the women started to act as if they'd just gone from business attire to cocktail, though they hadn't changed their clothes. It was transformative. This made me feel like Hair Blinger was going to be a wonderful product for women in more ways than one.

I'd seen this happen a few times on my journey, one in particular I'll never forget. A few weeks before we were in Dallas, Patrice had helped me get my first retail sale in Delaware with this darling shop called Heart & Home. (Why I didn't think of this actual sale when Nate from Walmart asked me if I'd sold it anywhere else, God only knows.)

After the owners placed an order with me, I got a little loud and excited in the store and hugged them both—my typical cool and subtle reaction to things. A few minutes later, one of the saleswomen asked me what the commotion was about. I told her about my product, then asked, "Do you want me to bling your hair?"

"Sure," she said, and I popped five Swarovski crystals in her hair. Her eyes lit up when she looked in the mirror.

"Oh my gosh, I love this!" she said, as if I'd just placed diamonds in her hair. Then she quickly looked back into the mirror. "I hated how my hair looked this morning," she said, her eyes now getting glassy as she started to tear up. "But now I feel so pretty. Thank you so much. You made my day!" It was astounding the effect it had.

Now it was happening in front of us again.

After a while, the crowd started heading down to the cocktail party in the lobby. Patrice and I headed to our last pitch with Spinmaster. They showed some interest, but it wasn't as hot or as energetic as what we'd received from others. I think everyone was tired at that point. We didn't let it sway us though. We felt it had been truly an amazing day.

Little did we know how much more amazing it was about to get.

We were practically the last ones to leave the floor, and we were hungry and tired. We couldn't wait to get to the cocktail reception in the lobby. As we came around the corner from the elevators, I noticed people were pointing in our direction.

I turned around to see who had come in behind us, but no one was there. That's when I realized, they were pointing at us. All I could think was *Oh my Lord!*

Of course we had just blinged up thirty to forty women, and they were all there. It had caught fire. We had become the talk of Empowerment Day.

Within moments I was surrounded. I hadn't even made it into the party area, and I had people calling out and pointing at me over the ropes, saying things like, "Hey, I need to talk to you."

Once we got in, I couldn't move. People were pulling on my arm, blocking my path, asking me, "Do you have a second?" I didn't want to be rude, so I stayed put and spoke to everyone who approached me.

The whole night was like that. I couldn't eat; I couldn't drink. So many people talking to me, wanting me to talk to someone they knew, to take their card and call them about XYZ. They were lining up, and some were even getting impatient. One woman held up her hand to another lady that was looking like she might be buttin' in and said, "You need to give me a few minutes," in a "back off" kind of way.

In my head, I was saying, *Oh my gosh, that's not nice.* I gave the other woman an "I'm so sorry" look.

Stefanie Barone came up at one point and told me, "Take it all in, but don't worry. We'll talk tomorrow." She was reassuring and calm. There was no pressure from her. She was definitely part of the reason I liked Wicked Cool Toys.

I met so many wonderful people who were just excited about my product and wanted to hear my story, who I was and where I came

Even Jason was in on the blinging action at the cocktail reception!

from. Vincent Imaoka, one of the speakers on the panel that morning with Hasbro, and his lovely wife, Shizuka, came up to me, and Vincent said she was interested in seeing Blinger. She was so sweet I couldn't help but ask her if she wanted her hair blinged. She did, and so I broke it out again right in the middle of the cocktail reception.

Empowerment Day created a lot of buzz for Hair Blinger and put it on the map. It was a significant and huge part of finally being successful on my journey. It gave me the opportunity to meet with the biggest toy buyers in the world and the possibility of partnering with some amazing toy companies, if I wanted to take that route.

It also gave me something to think about.

Did I want to continue down the road of self-producing? Or would I be better off licensing it to a bigger toy company, who could help make my dream a reality quicker and with a lot less risk on my side? I felt I had options and that I could have my pick of what was best for my product now. It was an incredible feeling. And I mean good when I say incredible here. The whole experience was surreal.

You can't just walk into Dallas or New York Toy Fair as a new inventor and get these kinds of personal one-on-one meetings with these companies. Empowerment Day is essential for any inventor who has an idea for a toy. I would say it is *the* event to attend to make your dream a reality.

It had taken me more than four years to get to this point, with a series of failures that were actually not failures it turned out, but crucial stepping-stones:

- I didn't get fully funded on my second Kickstarter—*fail.*
- But ASTV found me via that Kickstarter and wanted to license my product, so I learned all about tooling and manufacturing, plus I had time to focus on my children during a tough family time—*win!*
- But they couldn't make the product work properly and the deal ended—*fail.*
- *Funderdome* found me via that same Kickstarter and brought me on the show—*win!*
- But I lost to Hose Hooker—*fail.*
- Then my *Funderdome* show aired a year later—*win!*
- But I hardly got any sales from it—*fail.*

- But an established toy company saw my appearance on *Funderdome* and wanted to license my product—*win!*
- But the deal fell apart—*fail.*
- But then I got $10,000 from that toy company, which allowed me to hire my fifth engineering firm, who finally made the best prototype, the Blinger we sell today—*double win!*
- And it was through discussions with that toy company that I learned of Dallas Toy Fair and then because of what happened with that, namely Walmart showing interest the *day before* Dallas Toy Fair had started, that brought me to Empowerment Day and the incredible, indescribable moment of having a room full of people loving my product, which led to me finally realizing my dream—*biggest win ever!*

There you have it. While I didn't see it at the time, all these failures were directly connected to each other and led to Hair Blinger finally becoming a success! That day all tracked back to my failed Kickstarter in 2016.

As I've said before, don't be afraid of failure. It's the quickest way to learn anything and the only way to the top. Don't think of failure as a bad thing. Instead, try to think of it as a success-navigation system—a series of necessary waypoints along your journey to make your dream come true.

And, as we believers all know and understand, through failure is where God does his greatest work within us. He had a plan, and in time it was revealed.

That night, after crashing for a couple of hours, I woke up and spent a few hours making more discs by hand because we had used up so many that day—I was already having to replenish stock, and the show hadn't even started yet.

I was still in shock over all that had happened that day. October 1, 2018, was the day our lives were forever changed. If I hadn't gone to that WIT event, I might never have met WCT or Walmart, nor gotten the flurry of excitement I received for my product. Those curtained-off meetings, what Mary Kay did—all of it was absolutely crucial to having the opportunities that came next. Otherwise I might have been just another booth in the maze of thousands of booths. I might have or might not have met the WCT folks. But even if I had, I probably wouldn't have had a private pitch with Michael and Jeremy. I probably wouldn't have even been noticed by the Walmart buyers. It was a day I'll never forget.

For me, everything was riding on this week being successful, and thankfully it was off to a great start.

When we walked into the World Trade Center the next morning, women started pointing at us again. I looked over my shoulder for the second time in twelve hours to see who was behind me. I couldn't believe they were pointing at us. It was so incredible. (You know the kind of incredible I mean here!)

I heard one say, "There they are!" Then they came up and asked us where our booth was.

I was just like, *Oh my gosh!*

Most all the women from WIT came by that day too, mainly to hang out and see how we were, but also to support us and to give us more advice. It was awesome. Many team members from WCT also came by. It felt like the whole company was courting me. Stefanie bought her Hair Blinger for forty dollars and told me not to tell anyone. I made her sign an NDA and told her not to tell anyone too. I had to be a little shrewd. I mean, she was taking my device and worked for a competitor!

At one point, Michael came and whisked me away to the WCT booth. I grabbed Jason, who had come back to Dallas the night before to help us out. I really liked WCT's booth. The people, the ambience. There was a lot of energy and fun, as it should be with a cool up-and-coming toy company. Their booth had a manned check-in station outside the door. You had to be approved to enter their showroom and see their new toys. I saw this was how most of the big toy companies were set up, I guess for protection from other companies stealing ideas. (I know it's sad to think that companies that make toys for children could be this way, but it happens.)

After a tour of the new products they were launching for 2019, Michael took Jason and me into one of the private internal conference areas. I shared more of my story with him, telling him about all the engineers I went through, and all the time and money I invested to finally just get a feasible working prototype. Then, how I'd sold our home to build the tool in China. I told him about how hard it had been being a mom of four by day then overseeing manufacturing by night—but how grateful I was that I went for it.

At one point, Jason said, "Hey, Patrice wants us to come back to the booth," but this was just as Michael had started to share his own story, about how a few years earlier, WCT had been really close to closing their doors—but how they made it through and were doing great now. Michael started to tear up while he was sharing this with me, and any time someone starts to cry, that makes me cry. I put my hand on his.

Then Jason said again, "I hate to interrupt, but we really need to get back to our booth."

I looked at him like, *Uh, hello. This CEO guy we barely know is crying over how his company nearly failed. I'm not going to leave him right now.* I said, "It's okay, Jason. Whatever it is, it can wait."

"It's Walmart."

I dropped Michael's hand. "Sorry, we gotta go."

We ran back to our booth, which thankfully was on the same floor. When we came around the corner, we saw Brandon with two other Walmart buyers, one of whom I was sure was Lisa.

Patrice told us later that she'd asked them to come back when we weren't there the first time, and apparently Lisa had said, "We'll come back, but I don't usually come back." As it turned out, not only had she come back, she'd waited.

I immediately apologized for making her wait, then jumped into the booth and got on with the demo, which was essentially blinging Patrice's hair and then brushing it out while sharing bits of my story.

This was it. Walmart, for goodness' sake, was there to judge if we were good enough to be on their shelves. This was my opportunity to win or lose, and I wasn't going to lose if I could help it.

As I showed them how the product worked, I shared my pitch: my story, my passion, and my belief. I wanted Lisa, the most powerful toy buyer in the whole world, to know that I wouldn't let her down if she ordered even one Hair Blinger from me. She seemed *maybe* interested. It was tough to know with her. I respected that.

After the demo, they gave us some recommendations, one being that they wanted to see multiple colors on the same disc. I told them we could do that. In the end it appeared to be a pretty positive meeting.

I'm a hugger, if you haven't picked up on that. I like to give 'em and get 'em. Lisa Bowman, for the record, is not a hugger. Huggers can tell who is and who isn't. But I have more boldness than sense sometimes, so I went right in and hugged her anyway. It would have felt rude if I hadn't. Everyone laughed about it, but I hoped I wasn't being too brave.

First day of Dallas Toy Fair, in my booth, October 2, 2018.

As the first day wore on, others started to tell us that we were the talk of the show. Rob Mendelson, VP of sales with Farm Hoppers, who was in the booth next to mine, popped his head around every so often to give us a little tip or high five. He was excited for us. "You're like Rainbow Loom when they came here," he told us. "You're going to be toy of the year!"

I was so in awe, but I tried to stay focused. Then the energy started changing in our booth and began to feel more like trepidation.

I have heard that excitement and fear are pretty much identical emotions, two sides of the same coin, and we were starting to hear actual warnings from some of the people who stopped by. How everyone knew we were small. Shoot, I'd shared my story with every single person I'd demoed the product for. Single mom, sold my home to manufacture the product, just got the product in on Saturday... I thought at the time sharing these things would be a way of connecting with others, being relatable, and it was, but it was also possibly making myself and the company seem vulnerable and potentially an easy target.

Because of that, I started to consider licensing—as not only a way to partner up with people who understood how to produce and market Hair Blinger better, but also to protect us from being demolished. I knew how quickly the toy companies could move—I'd seen it firsthand the year before with the other toy company that had wanted to license with me. Better to have a small slice of pie than no pie at all.

Michael told me whatever I decided, he would help me—even if I decided to go with another company. That made me like them even more. Plus, he wasn't pressuring me, and he clearly had a heart and a great sense of humor, which was big for me.

That night, I called Glenn. "We need to file the international patent. Like *today*." Glenn was blown away by everything that had happened in only two days and was just so excited for me.

I had gone to Dallas for three reasons: 1) to meet with Walmart; 2) to gain feedback about my product from retailers; and 3) to get sales. I managed to do all those things, but I came to realize the sale I was really going to get was probably not going to be with a retailer. We were too small, young, and inexperienced. We had a way to go to be able to deliver a quality product to any retailer, let alone a Target or a Walmart.

I decided that licensing Hair Blinger was the right move. When we got back to Delaware, I was pretty sure I was going to license with Wicked Cool Toys, but only for a portion of the marketplace; I was going to hold on to the salon, bridal, cheer, and teen segment—the women's market.

Exactly one week after the WIT event, we met in their offices in Bristol, Pennsylvania, only an hour and a half from where I lived. Exactly one week after that, we had a deal memo with all our terms outlined and in place for our eventual agreement.

They would have Blinger, a toy product, and I would have Hair Blinger, a product for teens and women. This is how we agreed to divvy up the market space. The next day they left for Hong Kong's Toy Fair, ready to present their new product, Blinger, to the world.

Chapter 18

"Don't shine so that others can see you, shine so that through you, others can see Him."

~*C. S. Lewis*

Almost as soon as Michael got to Hong Kong, he started calling me late at night (morning there). His first call was to tell me that I was the next Lady Spanx! That everyone was going crazy for Blinger, and just sharing his excitement. The next night, it was about how so many of his distributors wanted to know if they had an adult version of the product for the beauty retailers they also represented. At first he told them, "No, this is all we have. We're a toy company."

But by the fifth or sixth person to ask, he decided that he should look into this with me, and that he would help me. "There's definitely a market for Hair Blinger," he told me.

"I know!" I said, and added, "I think it's the bigger market, in fact."

On November 2, 2018, I got a text from Glenn saying that we'd gotten a notice of allowance for the patent. Basically this meant that my patent had been approved and was going to be issued sometime in the next few months. Notice anything special about the date I was told this? What are the odds that exactly four years to the day of my dream, I would find out I was getting the patent? It's not odds, it's God! He loves to show up and knock us over with a feather.

While Blinger was being shopped around the world, I was working with my factory and getting excited for our second shipment after Dallas, which was part of our first official order. Thanks to my advance on royalties from WCT, I was keeping the Hair Blinger side of my business going and was able to keep paying Kimmie. Kind of important since she'd just had her baby, Olivia Jane. The company's first Blinger baby.

We had two big orders to fulfill for Christmas: those from our 2017 Kickstarter campaign and those for our first retail customer, Heart & Home.

In early December, our Kickstarter order arrived. It was like Christmas had come early. It was so exciting. We tested the devices and a few of the Swarovski discs, and everything worked perfectly. We were thrilled!

Our Kickstarter had only Swarovski crystals as an option. And we didn't need to provide retail packaging, which was good, because China wasn't ready with putting our product in packaging yet (except for our small Heart & Home order).

We bought little baggies for all the discs and small boxes with teal crinkle paper for the device. We made labels with our logo for the baggies and the boxes. Then we printed thank-you cards and instructions. We were ready.

Our fulfillment center was my already jam-packed townhome. All my kids were involved with the sorting of disc colors, packaging them in the correct baggies, and loading the Hair Blingers, either teal or black, into the boxes. Grace, who was only five, loved filling all the boxes with the crinkle paper. She was really good at it too!

We fulfilled every order without a hitch. *Ahh. Finally.*

Our retail plan for our website, and all retailers, was to offer two options, a rhinestone starter pack and a Swarovski starter pack. Each starter pack would come with the device and five discs—either rhinestone or Swarovski crystals.

A couple days later, we got our next shipment of 170 starter packs—160 rhinestone starter packs and ten Swarovski. Plus, we received 340 refill packs—three hundred rhinestone and forty

Swarovski crystals—all for Heart & Home. These were the only orders China was able to get to us in packaging before Christmas. The remaining forty-two hundred starter packs and over ten thousand refill packs would arrive in the new year to my teeny-tiny townhome.

Grace helping with fulfillment of our Kickstarter—stuffing the boxes with crinkle paper.

A completed Kickstarter box.

It was an incredible moment to see all the boxes arrive for our first retail sale. It finally felt like we were in business. I was ready to hit the road to sign up every salon on the Eastern Seaboard. Product development, testing, working out all the kinks—that was behind us. Kimmie and I both started crying. Everything was awesome. It was real, and we were making it happen.

Why is it that our greatest moments in life are sadly often short-lived?

Within about half an hour, I was crying again, but not tears of joy this time. More like desperate, questioning, and pathetic ones.

We had opened one of the rhinestone starter packs to test it and discovered it didn't work. Several of the stones would push through, but the glue stayed on the disc and the stones would fall to the floor. That was one issue. Another was that some stones just wouldn't come off the disc at all. Everything we tested was failing.

When we got to the refill packs, we had more issues. We realized whatever clear tape they'd used to keep the discs from moving around inside the packaging was too strong, so pulling the disc off would tear the packing behind the tape as well, and we couldn't get that tape and the torn packaging to come off the discs. That issue we knew we could fix, either using a less bionic tape or even laying the discs in a tray without tape at all. The bigger issue was that only three to five of fifteen rhinestones would push off the disc and go onto the hair.

Why had everything been okay with the Dallas discs, and the Kickstarter ones too? What was going on with these? Was the cold weather affecting the glue? Did they use the correct glue? Was it a change in the process of how they were making the discs at the factory? I immediately got on the phone with Vishaal, made videos for our manufacturer, and left messages for our glue reps (where we bought our glue that we shipped to China). Even after a week of meetings and discussions, no one had a viable answer for me.

One afternoon during this time, when she got home from school, Cambria asked me what was wrong. I think she noticed my eye twitch had come back. "Just the issues that came out of nowhere with the product, and if we don't get it figured out," I explained, gesturing to the row of boxes lined up along our hallway, "all these Hair Blingers are useless."

What I didn't tell her was that in my heart, I was also worried about my new deal with WCT. At this point, we only had a deal memo in place. Not the final agreement. They had advanced me money too. I was genuinely concerned I might lose the deal. My third licensing deal to fall through.

I wanted to talk to Michael, but I didn't want to talk to Michael. Maybe the product was working for him, like it had for us in Dallas. I didn't want to draw attention to a problem until I knew what exactly the problem was and at least had a clue on how to solve it. But at the same time, I really wanted his advice.

I didn't call. I decided I was going to figure this out on my own, by the grace of God, like I'd done so many times before.

When I told Cambria how I just didn't get why the rhinestone packs didn't work when the Swarovski discs had been fine, she suggested, "It must be something about the rhinestones, then."

"No," I said chuckling. "It's not the rhinestones, sweetie." I tried to respond without sounding condescending. She's so smart, but that was such a cute kid response. "Something about the rhinestones."

Wait a minute!

It hit me like a bolt. Images flashed through my mind, and suddenly I remembered clearly and vividly the differences I'd seen all these years from working with these stones. I darted into the kitchen and grabbed a couple of the discs and compared the underside of the rhinestones to the underside of the Swarovski crystals. There it was. She was right. The rhinestones' coating under the stone was shiny and slick, while the underside of Swarovski crystals is matte, with a coarser texture—so the glue stays on the crystals but slides off the rhinestones. She called it simply and clearly. It had something to do with the rhinestones. That's my Cam.

Holy Hannah! I thought. My fourteen-year-old daughter had just figured out what our Chinese manufacturer and several Chinese engineers, my mechanical engineer, two experts in glue, and I had not.

My next step was to see if we could source rhinestones with a coarse undercoating, but Janice soon informed us they couldn't find any supplier that made them like that. So we had to figure out how to make the product work with shiny rhinestone bottoms.

First, I learned that, though Vishaal had done tons of testing with rhinestones, it had been with rhinestones from the craft store, which have a different glue on them, not our hair-safe glue. The only stones he'd tested with our glue were the ASTV strips, all Swarovski crystals. This explained why we didn't have these issues in testing the rhinestones during development, remember, we had done a boatload.

Over the next couple of weeks, after a lot of calls, emails, testing, and shipments back and forth between China, Chicago, and Delaware, we eventually figured out two solutions that made the product work better with rhinestones. One was to add silicone to both sides of the disc. Next, we made a tiny two-millimeter hole in the center of each star cutout on the disc, so that only the rim of the rhinestones would be touching the edge of the disc cutouts. Both of these solutions helped to keep the glue more on the rhinestone and less on the disc and thus made getting the rhinestone off the disc easier when pushed.

Unfortunately, we were still only getting about an 80 percent efficiency rate. Better, but not good enough. I had learned that in product development, it's rarely ever 100 percent, and that you can launch a product with a 95 percent performance rating and probably be okay. For us that would mean out of seventy-five stones, five discs with fifteen stones on each, it wouldn't hurt us with the consumer if three stones in a refill pack didn't work for some reason. But we weren't getting three out of seventy-five, we were getting fifteen out of seventy-five not working. On average, three stones per disc, three stones per fifteen, were failing. Not acceptable.

What were we missing? What else could we do?

I thought, *there's four parts to this equation: the disc, the glue, the stone, and the plunger.*

The plunger is the part of the device that pushes the stone off the disc out onto the hair or other surface you want to bling. I turned the device over in my hand and looked at it. It looked like a pretty basic piece—small and plastic with a hole in the middle. Nothing very aesthetic or special. Just a tiny plastic tube. Then I realized you could place a three-millimeter crystal, the top part of it, perfectly in the hole. It fit so well, it could get stuck in there.

It occurred to me that this might be why we did have trouble with the three-millimeter crystals on occasion. I hadn't worried about that just yet because WCT wasn't planning on doing the small stones for the toy space. The small crystals were much more important for the women's market, to give a delicate but dazzling effect in the hair, beautiful and more subtle. But I was just going to launch with only four-millimeter and up crystals until I had resolved that issue I'd seen. It also occurred to me that because the plunger was plastic, it could possibly slide on some stones if they weren't perfectly centered on the disc. That's when I had an idea.

I found one of my children's pencils and tore off the eraser. Then I dug out the middle with a safety pin. That took half an hour! I slid the gutted eraser over the plunger, then secured it in place with Scotch tape.

I then loaded a disc into the device and blinged fifteen rhinestones onto a piece of paper in no time flat. My heart did a back flip. Maybe it was a fluke? *Do it again,* I said to myself. I loaded another disc and blinged fifteen more stones onto the paper. Then I tried it in my hair. Fifteen stones flawlessly placed on my hair in a matter of seconds. Hallelujah!

I was so excited I called Vishaal but got his voice mail. I had to rush out and get one of my kids from school, but when I hadn't heard back from him after an hour passed, I called again. He picked up this time.

"Hey! Did you hear my message!" I practically shouted.

"Oh, what about the eraser?"

"Yes, *about the eraser!*" I replied, dumbfounded. "I think the rubber is what we've been missing."

"Not sure. Maybe. I'll take a look at your prototype and go from there, I guess."

"What? You can make one now! Don't you have a pencil with an eraser on it?"

"Okay, I'll try it," he said.

Three hours later, he texted me a picture with an eraser on the plunger and asked, "Like this?"

Vishaal's eraser placed around the plunger (without scotch tape).

"Yes! Perfect!" I replied.

He wrote back, "Oh, it just gets stuck." Then he sent me a video of the eraser plunger getting stuck closed in the hole it passes through and not popping back up as it should.

Oh my gosh. What was going on? I was so frustrated. Did he think I was making up my results? Could he not think to maybe slim down his eraser so it wouldn't get stuck? *He's an engineer, for goodness' sake! And a good one at that.*

I don't think I'm too insecure, but I don't have a degree in engineering, so it was hard to not feel a little apprehensive telling an engineer how to engineer something. If I was an engineer and someone did that, it would have seemed a little arrogant to me anyway, but I was staring at the problem every day. He wasn't. I had 160 rhinestone devices in packaging and three hundred rhinestone refill packs (remember the Swarovski items all worked) strewn all over my house for the two to three weeks we'd all been working on this, and all worthless if we couldn't solve it. I had already accepted that my first sale to Heart & Home was not happening. But I was not going to lose WCT too, if I could help it.

Up until that moment, Vishaal and I had gotten along great. He was awesome to work with, and he did what no one else had. I didn't want to be upset with him. But I was beside myself. As calmly as possible, I texted back. "Shave off the sides some...that eraser is probably thicker than mine or something. Put tape around it to make it smoother on the sides, so it won't get stuck."

And then I sent an extra text—like I've warned you *not* to do when you're upset—asking him, "Why are you fighting me on my idea?"

He wrote back, "I'm not fighting your idea. I'm simply telling you I'm not getting the same results."

I felt bad. I hate when I send mean texts or emails. I apologized immediately then nicely suggested, again, "Try shaving down the eraser and put clear tape around it to make it slick" with a smiley emoji.

He said he would try and get back to me.

Within an hour, he wrote back, "Yes okay. I'm getting good results. I think this could be our winner. Will keep testing. I think we're on the right track now."

A couple hours later, he wrote, "Seems to even work with misaligned gems. This is nice. Also, trust me, I don't care where the ideas come from as long as this gets figured out. I didn't realize you had tape around the rubber."

To write this next part brings tears to my eyes.

I stood up for what I knew was right. It was great that I came up with the eraser idea, but it was that I fought for it that made me realize on that day, December 20, 2018, why God chose me. I didn't back down. I had failed so many times on my journey, that even after the success in Dallas, I didn't get why he chose me. But at that moment, I felt fairly certain that I was the only person who could have done this. Not bragging. Not saying I'm great. I'm just saying that I'm not afraid to get into the ring and battle, even after being pummeled by one engineer after the other. And that I don't give up probably also helps. I was just so happy and clear at that moment that despite all my doubts, it seemed I was the right choice for this after all. Maybe I took a little longer than he thought, but he knew I would get there.

This small change to the plunger took us all the way home and also improved efficiency with our Swarovski crystals.

I knew that now was the time to talk to Michael. We had some engineering left to do with this change, but at least I was bringing a solution to him, not just a problem. When we got on the phone, after exchanging pleasantries, I said, "I have something to tell you."

Then I told him everything that had happened in the past three weeks since we got the product. The whole thing with Vishaal, China, Cambria, the glue factory, and that I had wanted to reach out to him many times, but that I didn't want to bring him the problem until I figured it out or at least gave it my best shot. I told him that we had discovered and resolved the problem. But that we were going to need some time to revise some of the design files for the plunger and to the discs, and that we would get it to him as soon as they were completed.

Michael got unusually quiet while I spoke. I was afraid he was thinking, *Oh gosh, what is this woman telling me?* I stopped talking and waited, holding my breath, sitting on my hands.

He said, "Angie, I've had our people in China working on this problem for over a month now, and you figured it out," he said. "All these engineers couldn't solve it, and you did it. I need you to go to China."

Chapter 19

"Your strength doesn't come from winning. It comes from struggles and hardship. Everything that you go through prepares you for the next level."

~**Germany Kent**, American print and broadcast journalist

In early 2019, Cambria and I had been invited to help work the WCT booth at New York Toy Fair at the end of February. We loved being there and had the best time working it together.

Cambria and me representing Blinger in Wicked Cool Toys' booth, New York Toy Fair, February 2019.

The Blinger section of their booth blew me away. What they had done with the product in a few short months would have taken Kimmie, Jason, and me years. I don't know if we would have even gotten that far. They had packaging done in other languages. We couldn't even get our packaging done quickly or correctly in English, let alone Korean or French. And of course, they had created a new logo, rebranding it back to Blinger. It was the first of many confirmations that I had made the right decision for all of us.

Fifth logo.

Herb Mitschele, senior VP of global sales with WCT, who is like the cherry on top of all my new besties at WCT, was talking to a distributor in front of Cam and Zyta, Michael's beautiful wife, while I was blinging away. He said, "This is a product that will not only kill it for you, but it's a product you'll feel good about buying because of Angie's story."

I stopped blinging. I started to tear up. "Aw, thank you," I told him, trying not to cry in front of everyone. Sometimes things just hit you out of nowhere, and they're strong and meaningful. My story was a mess to me, and here he was bragging about it. Such a turnaround from then to now. I needed to keep myself together though, so I tried to make a joke. "I'm just hoping we'll sell enough to get us out of our townhome."

Jeremy had walked up just then and said, "Angie, you're gonna be able to buy five homes with Blinger, not just one. You'll be able to get one for yourself and each of your kids!"

Cam's eyes lit up. She loved hearing that! I was so thankful for all of it and thanked God under my breath.

We just loved blinging people at the show. Plus we met so many celebrities—famous YouTubers, like Natalie Clark with Toys Unlimited, Alana and fam with DavidsTV, Emma and Mila Stauffer, the Tic Tac Toy family, Melissa Hunter, Toy Daycare, and my now very good friend, whom Cambria and I fell in love with at first sight, Princess T (yes, children everywhere, Princess T and I are friends!), and other just fun, cool influencers in different spaces, including some famous toy inventors too. It was a blast—just like a toy fair should be!

A group of about twenty inventors were being escorted through the booth. These inventors are shown all the toy products with all the toy companies at these events and then asked to come up with ideas to expand on them and grow the lines. All white men, by the way. Like, zero diversity. (Hint, hint, women of all colors everywhere and nonwhite men.)

One of the inventors, who had been the one to point out the lack of diversity in the toy inventor community, said, "We work hard every day and pitch several ideas a month to the toy companies just to get one to hit big like yours."

I was like "wow" and thanked him for sharing. Herb overheard him and yelled out, "Yeah, Ange, you can be one and done!"

As I mentioned earlier, the big toy companies don't want competitors seeing the inside of their booths, but people were lining up to come into WCT's booth, including employees of other toy companies. They were saying things like, "We won't look around, we promise. We just want to get our hair blinged." It was crazy, just like in Dallas, and I was thankful Cambria was there to experience the same excitement and commotion that I had seen.

It's hard to give up control, but it's harder to think about all I might have missed had I held on. I might have missed the chance to take my kids on a seven-day cruise and us staying in a suite. Going to Key West and eating whatever we wanted off the menu—"Sure, you can have steak, Grace!" Renting a lake cabin for a week, all of us just canoeing, fishing, and watching the sunset every night. Or I might have missed me being in all the pictures with them. Didn't miss a one this time.

Crystal Pizzullo was chosen as senior director of brand management for Blinger. She is an amazing woman who can juggle an infinite number of details and logistics like no one else ever.

Blinger was in the right hands with her and WCT, and I definitely made more by licensing Blinger than I would have had I tried to bring it into the market with my small team. Of course, my team is phenomenal, but we weren't toy experts and there weren't enough of us—like, we were ninety-eight people short. On top of that, I probably would have lost more in lawsuits fighting competitors copying my product than I'd have ever gained if I hadn't licensed to a company big enough to make it happen yet also small enough to move so quickly. Wicked Cool Toys was the perfect fit for me and Blinger.

Stefanie and me in China drinking our Starbucks, May 2019.

In May of 2019, I did go to China with my good buddy, Stefanie Barone, and had the amazing opportunity to visit the two factories where they were making the discs and devices. I was able to watch an automated machine that they'd modified and built for our discs make twelve of them in under a minute. That's when I knew

Blinger would be okay. All those years wondering what machine would be able to make the disc (or strip), and there it was. I cried.

This machine could make two hundred thousand discs a day, which was good but not enough. Even running nonstop, it could only produce six million discs a month. Between the two factories, we needed five hundred million (yes, I wrote that number right, half a billion) discs a month in order to cover all the orders by that August. They needed two more machines like this at both factories, six machines in all, and these machines were half a million dollars each. Yes, I cried. The sheer magnitude shocked me, and I was utterly thankful to God that this wasn't on my shoulders anymore.

Stefanie told me, "Angie, we wouldn't be able to launch this product and fulfill all these orders if you hadn't already proved it out by building the tool. We wouldn't be this far along—able to hit it this year. It would have been 2020 if we had had to start from prototype."

It touched my heart and made me feel much less guilty about the gamble I took in selling our home to build that tool. It was pretty dramatic for us, the move, especially for my children, and around that time we had just come to terms with the fact that we had to renew the townhome for another year. Her sharing that with me made the whole downsizing part, that sacrifice, not only tolerable but gave it even more meaning and significance.

We decided, as a family, since we were going to be in our townhome another year, that we might as well build our dream home. I found some land that came with a builder, hired an architect, and drew up the plans. In our new home, everyone will have their own bedroom and bathroom. We're putting an indoor soccer field in the basement, and I've got my very own custom prayer room—war room—right next to my closet.

To say I'm grateful that Blinger was successful, and in such a big, amazing way, is an understatement. All the pain and struggle ended up being worth it. And just to have people stop looking at me like I was this crazy loon—very fulfilling.

> *"The distance between insanity and genius is measured only by success."*
>
> ~**Bruce Feirstein**, American screenwriter and humorist

But if we hadn't had this success, if it hadn't turned out this way, we would have been fine, because happiness is wherever the five of us are. Townhome or dream home, it doesn't matter. We were already successful.

TIPS FOR WHEN YOU MAKE IT

- **Give God the glory.**
- **Be grateful.** Know it's by the grace of God you're here.
- **Keep a servant's heart.** Be there for others who might love to be where you are and help them get where they want to go.
- **Be humble.** Don't let your title, newfound fame, or fortune define you. Stay you. Find your identity in Christ and this will not be a problem.
- **Be a role model.** Be a good example to others of what success looks like. People are watching you now.
- **Be generous.** Have some fun. Grab everyone who supported you and whom you love and spoil them. They may have missed you and need extra attention now. Give it to them.
- **Help others.** Remember your bigger purpose and meaning for the goal. Take care of any sacrifices you made and then make that your focus. Give back.

Chapter 20

"All things are possible to the person who believes."

~*Jesus*, Mark 9:23

Before I went to China in May, I brought Evan and Grace with me to a WCT meeting, as they were both under the weather and not in school that day—but not too sick to go to a toy company. I learned during that meeting that WCT had not only built another tool, but twelve of them. I mentioned to Michael, "I thought a tool would outlast the life of a product. Why do you need so many?"

He explained, "Angie, the tool can only produce so many plastic parts in a single day. To meet demand, we needed to build more."

"Wow." I sat there in shock. So glad I wasn't responsible for building twelve more tools. I could barely afford the one.

That wasn't all. I also learned that Blinger was going to be on two endcaps with Target and one with Walmart, possibly two. This was also a big deal that I didn't get initially.

As we drove back home that afternoon, I called Cambria and shared how incredible the meeting was and about all the endcaps, but she wasn't responding with much enthusiasm. (Kinda like me in the meeting. Everyone had gasped when Bob Turner, VP of sales, announced it over the big Skype screen, and I was just sitting there, like do-to-do-to-do. It meant nothing to me.) So I asked her, "Do you know what an endcap is, Cam?"

"No."

"It's the shelves at the end of the aisle, where they put products for you to see when you walk by the aisles."

"Oh, you mean where they have all the clearance items?"

"No, honey, that's where we shop. These are on the front end of the aisle, that face out into the main walkway, where all the full-price items are!"

"Ohh, that's cool!"

"Michael said that in thirty years of being in toys, they've only had three other endcaps. None of them in the same year, none of them with the same product, and none with a brand-new product."

"Oh my gosh, Mama!"

"I know! This is crazy! I need to write my book so it can be sitting there on display next to all these endcaps!"

She asked me what she could do, which was so sweet, because teenagers don't often ask what they can do to help their mamas.

I suggested, "Maybe google top ten book publishers in New York and send me that list?"

Within minutes I had a list from Cambria. For some reason, I decided to call the second one, RosettaBooks. When their voice mail system came on, asking me to enter an extension for the person I was calling, I just entered random numbers on my car's phone display, since I was driving and had no idea whom I wanted to talk to. It actually connected me to a real person, a gentleman, and I began talking quickly about what I was hoping to do.

He said, "Look, if you're looking for a publisher or an agent, I'm not interested."

I told him, "I don't know what I'm looking for...my product is going to be on all these endcaps and I just think I have a story here and want to have my book there next to my product."

He said, "This is too abstract. I can't really discuss this right now, it's too abstract over the phone. Here's my email." He gave me his email, which I had Evan, sitting in the back seat, jot down for me. "Send me an email. This is too abstract to do this way." And he hung up.

The next day, I looked him up and found out the guy I spoke to, Arthur Klebanoff, was the CEO of RosettaBooks. I could not believe I had spoken directly to the CEO, and that he'd given me his email. I know I've bragged quite a bit about being a brave saleslady, but I was petrified of emailing this guy. I hadn't done corporate sales in over a decade. And what did I know about pitching a publisher?

It took me a week to get my nerve up. There's a window of opportunity and then it closes. Plus, it's weird when you wait too long, like what you had to share wasn't that important after all. And then, people just plainly forget too. It was now or never.

Before I sent Arthur an email, I tried to remember the word he kept repeating. I finally remembered it and my opening line to him was, "I hope this is less abstract." Then I gave him two or three paragraphs of my last four years and what was coming. It was intimidating writing to someone who reviewed writing for a living. But he replied right away, and by the next day, after a long discussion about books and publishing, he offered to take me on. We had an agreement within a couple weeks. When he realized, after a couple months, that not much was happening, he paired me with an amazing collaborator and editor, Francine LaSala. Francine and I are best buds now. She knows everything about my life and still likes me, so I had no choice but to love her in return.

When I later spoke with others who knew a thing or two about book publishing, I was told that this kind of thing never happens. That getting a book in front of a publisher is usually a huge, grueling process. It's hundreds of rejections. One day I was chatting with Christina Hayford, NVP with Arbonne, and her husband, Marc, radio host and author of three books. Both are believers and good friends of mine, and after sharing all that was going on, Marc said to me, "This *really isn't you* making all this happen, is it?"

I said, "Nope. That's what I've been saying. It's all God. I have little to do with a lot of this."

Wicked Cool Toys allowed me to put a picture of my kids and me on the packaging, along with a blurb about my journey—including giving thanks to God. This was the first time anyone had allowed me to profess my faith or even to give him a little credit. I was so thankful.

We had to get a group photo where everyone looked decent. On the way to the photographer's studio, Evan asked, "Hey, Mom, does my hair look good enough to be on millions of packages?" We all cracked up. He's so cute and funny—and clever.

Created by our Mom!

Blinger™ came to me in a dream that began a wild 4-year journey. Thanks to my wonderful children, amazing Mom, and faith in God, I brought Blinger™ to life for ALL of you. May you always shine brightly!

♡ Angie Cella

Angie Cella, Blinger™ Inventor

We're famous!

One day, Crystal let me know that Costco was doing a Blinger order. "Oh, that's nice," I said.

"No. You don't understand. Costco never buys new products. They only buy products with a track record that have been around forever."

"Really? Wow! That is something, then."

"On top of that, they usually get 150,000 units, but their order is for 225,000. It's so much more than normal, the sales rep called them back to make sure the number they sent was accurate."

"Wow. Amazing!"

"Here's the thing though. They don't want your story on the packaging. They will only accept your photo and 'Created by Our Mom,' with your signature."

"So they're basically taking God off the packaging? Is that what it is?" I asked.

"Yes, I'm sorry. They are adamant that we can't have it on there. We even pushed because we know how much it means to you."

"That's okay. I appreciate you trying. And thanks for letting me know."

Costco was the only one out of thirty-two American retailers that year who carried Blinger that was disappointed with their sales of the product, and they were the only ones that left God off the packaging. I wasn't surprised. I mean, of anyone to not mess with, or leave off, I'd say it's God.

On October 1, 2019, Jazwares, a company I had pitched at the WIT event exactly one year before, who had told me they didn't see my product being a fit for them, merged with WCT. A company five times WCT's size and backed by one of the biggest holding companies, Alleghany Capital, had bought them for millions of dollars, and Michael told me that Blinger was what had made that deal happen. I know it wasn't just Blinger, but it felt amazing to think my little product could help to make these other big things happen for someone else. I was thrilled.

RETAILERS WHO CARRIED BLINGER IN 2019

US and Canada:

AAFES
Amazon
Barnes & Noble
BJ's
Blain Supply, Inc.
Bluestem Brands
Claire's
Colony Brands
Costco
Fred Meyer
Friend Smith (Puerto Rico)
Gordman's
Hammacher Schlemmer
HEB
Justice
Kmart
Kohl's
Lewis Drug
Mason Company
Meijer
Michaels
Mills Fleet Farm
Party City
QVC
Scheels
Stage Stores
Target
Toys R Us Canada
Urban Outfitters
Veterans Canteen Service
Walgreens
Walmart
Zulily

International Stores and Distributors:

168 Marketing, Philippines
Anvol, Estonia
Bandai, France
Big Balloon, Australia
Costco, Australia
Bizak, Spain/Portugal
Black Fire, Czech Republic/Romania
Boti, Germany/Austria/Switzerland/Benelux
Camtec, Singapore
Character Options, UK
Cobi, Poland
Costco, Mexico
Happinet, Japan
Kade, Hong Kong
Kiddisvit, Ukraine
Mimi, Korea
New Toys, Brazil
Planet Fun, New Zealand
Pricesmart, Mexico
Proxy, Nordic

Over the summer I'd written bits and pieces here and there on my book. Lots of notes, not much substance. One of the things I had written however, that I thought was pretty good, I shared with Kimmie and Cambria one day:

"Many of us need to push our 'reset button' on who we think we are...and it should be set like this: I'm a precious child of the Most High God.

"And if I'm a child of God, then so are you. You are my sister or brother. Once all of us realize our value, we'll be able to realize the value of another. Until that happens, we're all stuck. Projecting our own negative views of ourselves out into the world."

Then, on Saturday, June 15, maybe a couple weeks after I had read that to them, I found myself alone, one of the first Saturdays in years that I was home without my children—no kids from noon on Saturday until Sunday night. I was so excited and I had big plans—I was going to write my book that weekend! It's so funny when you've never done something what kind of time you think it takes to do it.

Anyhoo, around three forty-five p.m., after my second Netflix movie and while staring at my Bible and laptop in shame, my phone started talking out of nowhere. A man's voice was just talking through it, like someone was on speaker. I picked it up and started closing windows. I closed everything, cleared all my notifications, but the man's voice was still playing. The sound wasn't even on.

Great! I thought, *Just when I was about to start writing* (right!) *now I have to go to the Apple store to get my phone fixed.*

After a few minutes, I realized the man was speaking words of faith, like on a podcast or something. Maybe this was a message I needed to listen to? I grabbed my notebook and started taking notes.

Part of the message that resonated with me was when he shared that we are *not* all God's children. That the only way to get into his family is by a second birth or adoption. And the only way to do that is through

Christ. By accepting his son as our Lord and savior, only then would we be God's child. When it ended, I learned it was a pastor named Richard Ellis who had been speaking.

To this point, I had had so much insecurity about writing a book about my faith. I mean, who was I to write about Jesus? We didn't make it to church many weekends. I hadn't even read the whole Bible. I felt ill equipped to share my thoughts about God with anyone, let alone potentially everyone.

So this message, coming out of nowhere through my phone, was, to me, God's way of making sure I got it right. I was so thankful. What I had written and just shared with my daughter and my friend was wrong, and he let me know. I felt much more confident that he was with me and wouldn't let me mess this up.

I couldn't wait to get to church the next day. As I ran toward the building, rushing as usual, a gentleman hurried to hold the door open for me. His name tag had Ward on it. I had an appointment with a Ward scheduled for the next day. I thanked him, then asked, "Are you the Ward with Covenant Wealth Strategies?"

"Yes," he said.

"Oh, I have a meeting with you tomorrow. I'm Angie Cella."

"Nice to meet you. What brings you to the church? Have you been here before?"

I explained that I had years ago, but then we'd moved to Pennsylvania. I told him that now that I was back in Delaware, I was hoping to find a church for me and my children and had decided to check them out again.

"Great," he said. "Welcome back."

"Thank you," I said, and then I felt compelled to tell him what had happened to me the day before. "I also had a weird experience yesterday with my phone. It just started playing a message from this pastor, Richard Ellis. Do you know him?"

"No."

"Oh. Well did anything play on *your* phone yesterday?"

"Uh, no," he replied, cautiously now.

"It was just so strange. I thought I'd better get to church today after that message played out of thin air."

"Yeah," he said as he was backing away.

"Do you want to know what the message was about?" I asked, moving toward him. Why I asked this, I have no idea. I normally don't keep talking to someone who clearly thinks I'm nuts. But I did.

He reluctantly said, "Sure." Then, when I told him about the message, he perked up, just a tiny bit, and said to me, "That's what today's service is about."

I almost knocked him to the floor. "What! Are you kidding!" *Who's the crazy one now?* I thought.

Then I rushed inside and sat down. The pastor did share the same message, and he also gave me further insight and understanding of it.

"We're all God's creation," he explained. "And we're all equally loved as his creation, but only those who follow Christ are considered his children."

Then he gave a great analogy. "Imagine you see the president of the United States and you start running toward him. What do you think will happen? You'll be stopped, tackled probably, or worse. But now imagine you're the president's child and you start running toward him. What will happen? You'll be let through. You'll have full access."

I was blown away. Not all of us have access, but we all can. I loved that. We have full access once we accept Jesus into our lives. My prayers work, and so can yours. Everything I want from my father, he gives me, I just have to ask. He's my secret weapon, and he can be yours too. Just invite him in.

He loves us and loves having a beautiful relationship with us. He desires more than anything in the world to have a relationship with you.

*"Keep on asking, and you will receive what you ask for.
Keep on seeking, and you will find. Keep on knocking,
and the door will be opened to you. For everyone who
asks, receives. Everyone who seeks, finds. And to everyone
who knocks, the door will be opened."*

~**Jesus,** Matthew 7:7–8

I was walking on air. *The Holy Spirit must love technology nowadays,* I thought. First being saved through my radio in 2012. Now making sure my book was accurate through my iPhone.

I went back home to write. I hadn't made much progress yet on that, and I knew I was losing time.

Then, at two p.m. on the dot, my phone started talking again. I ran to grab my notebook this time. Now, please don't freak out, but this message was about the end of times. And what that said to me wasn't something scary, but more how important it is that you get the first message. So, I'm just going to say this as boldly as I can. You need to accept Christ into your life. It is essential to your whole being, your eternal being.

*"I am the way, the truth and the life. No one can come to
the Father except through me."*

~**Jesus**, John 14:6

Once you accept him, you're in. You can't mess it up, either, so you don't need to be ready. Jesus has already died for all of our sins; he wants you as you are. And all you have to do is ask.

*"If you openly declare that Jesus is Lord and believe in
your heart that God raised him from the dead, you will
be saved. For it is by believing in your heart that you are
made right with God, and it is by openly declaring your
faith that you are saved."*

~**Romans** 10:9–10

That's it.

I asked for a purpose. He gave me an idea. I asked for direction. He gave me an adventure and a story. I asked for help for my children. He gave me a reprieve. I asked for a book. He gave me a publisher, an editor, and a friend. I asked for wisdom. He played me some podcasts.

What are you longing for? The desires of your heart are available to you.

Just ask.

I realized during the second message, from Greg Laurie, another pastor I didn't know, that it *was* a podcast. I rarely, if ever, listen to podcasts, I'd never heard of either of these guys, but I checked my podcast app to see if maybe I had downloaded them one night in my sleep. Neither his nor the one by Richard was ever downloaded or listed anywhere.

I watched the news that night and the next morning, wondering if this had happened to anyone else. I looked all over the internet. Nothing. Those two podcasts, not on my phone, not downloaded, not in my app, were apparently played—out of thin air—just for me.

Really, I think they were probably played for you.

I looked up the podcasts for this book and was further amazed. Richard's, called "Like Father, Like Son," played on June 15 but was not posted until June 16 on the podcast site. How did I hear it on the fifteenth? Greg's, called "What in the World Is Going On?" (appropriately—ha-ha!), was posted on the fourteenth, but it played the day after Richard's. Though posted in a different order, they played in the precise order that made the most sense for me to hear them.

The next morning, I started reading the book of Daniel in the Bible, the book Greg had talked about the most on his podcast. As I read, I saw that the book of Daniel was about dreams. Daniel was a dreamer.

I don't know what all this means. I'm seriously just a mom of four who had a dream about a product idea. I don't know why miracles happen, or why this happened to me. But miracles happen every day. I think we're just more distracted than ever before to actually see and experience them. But they are happening. And they seem to happen most when no one else is around. But I think why miracles happen in private is so that the rest of us get the choice to believe or not. It's all up to you—you choose what you want to believe.

In January 2020, Blinger was nominated for Toy of the Year and I was nominated for the Wonder Woman Award with WIT for Inventor of the Year. At the time of this writing, we've sold over $27 million wholesale worth of product, $60 million retail. I went from a dream, using all my savings, going more than $100,000 in debt, selling our home and risking another $120,000, and struggling for more than four years, to make that dream happen. And God made the dream much bigger than I had ever imagined.

Though it's changed our lives financially, I still feel like a mom on a budget. Just trying to keep it real for my kids and myself. I still say no on a daily basis to at least one of them. I didn't make this product to make money. I did it to meet Ellen and Oprah. Ha-ha!

Oh, and Dolly of course! *(Why doesn't she have a show?)*

Seriously, though, if I made money, that was just a byproduct. A good one, don't get me wrong—money is like oxygen, we all need it to survive—but it is just one aspect of achieving the goal. I'd like to think most inventors are thrilled with the challenge of solving the problem, that they're not just a driven or clever person trying to be rich.

Our greatest successes, I think, usually have little to do with money. That kind of success feels like nothing else in the world too. Finishing this last chapter has been more rewarding than getting my first check. It's the achievement. The success is in the accomplishment. The money is just the cherry on top, the icing on the cake, the crystal on the hair. (Sorry, you know I had to say it!)

When I get to heaven, I don't want to hear, "Way to go, Angie. You made a lot of cash. Great job." Sounds pretty empty, right? When I get to heaven, I want to hear my father say, "Well done, my good and faithful servant!" (~Jesus, Matthew 25:21) because I hopefully made a difference in someone else's life.

When I was younger, I was all about winning and being wealthy. Isn't that how we become somebody? I thought those things went hand in hand and would make me happy. But ask anyone who's "made it" and you'll find it didn't really change their happiness level. If there was emptiness before, the emptiness is still there. And many are confused when this happens. They had looked for their identity, their self-worth, and their happiness in things, people, titles, power, or money. Success and happiness come from something much bigger. Fulfillment in our lives, when we feel most satisfied, comes from meaning and purpose. And that's because we all have a God-given purpose, unique to ourselves. The goal is to discover what that is for you

For a while there, I started to find my identity in my title as inventor of Blinger. I got a little prideful. But I have come to realize that, ultimately, it does not and cannot define me. It is temporary, and the fulfillment that it brings is only if someone else knows and sees it as some great achievement, which then means my value is defined by it and what someone else thinks of it.

My identity is much deeper, much more meaningful to me than Blinger. My identity lies in Christ. "Fearfully and wonderfully made..." (Psalm 139:14). He guides my steps, sets my moral baseline, and gives me a framework to follow. He's my ultimate upline that I attempt to duplicate every day in my life.

If Christ were here today, he'd be with all the people our society rejects. I don't think he'd spend much time at church where many of us feel judged and no one is free to be in pain or messed up (not all churches are like this, by the way). He'd be with the least of us. He'd be wherever the suffering are. The poor, the imprisoned, the unforgiven, the rejected, and the lost. He came and showed love to the lepers, the prostitutes, the thieves, and the insane. And showed us that everyone matters to God—no one is worthless. That we all deserve love. And our biggest job is to love one another.

What Jesus taught me, and the world, about love is priceless. Love, the most powerful force in the universe, helps us find the right priorities for our life. Helps us to see what really matters. If you knew you were loved unconditionally, flaws and all, would you feel grateful? Relieved? Precious? Without Jesus how much would we really know about love?

And from love we find gratefulness for our lives and genuine success in our endeavors. Instantly we become more fulfilled. What fulfills you? For me it's about seeing something in my head become real. It can also be about helping others. How amazing do we feel when we do something special for a stranger or friend? But it can also be just getting four kids out the door at three different times to three different schools every morning and not losing my cool. That's real love and true success!

Success isn't about winning, it's about being, playing, win or lose, and never giving up. When we played games or sports as children, we were excited about the game or the goal for the goal's sake alone. Fulfillment came from the thrill of getting it across the finish line, being on a team with friends, high-fives and ice cream afterward. We played mostly because it was fun.

Success in life is the same. It is the life well played. And it begins with knowing that you're loved and what you do matters.

And what you do doesn't matter just to you. It may be life-changing for the rest of us. The world might not need a Blinger, but it does need exactly what you have to offer and that only you can bring into it. You're not replaceable, you're essential.

"God has given each of you a gift from his great variety
of spiritual gifts. Use them well to serve one another."

~*1 Peter* 4:10

Consider your life, your business, your aspirations like an adventure you're called to make. Don't sit idle, letting fear dictate your outcomes. Get in the game. Believe in your dreams. Find your faith, your purpose and begin your journey. The world needs you to shine and God is watching. Give him a good show.

> *"Many are the plans in a man's heart, but it is the Lord's purpose that prevails."*
>
> ~**Proverbs** 19:21

Acknowledgments

There are so many people I want to thank for helping me move through my journey to make Blinger and this book a reality. I didn't get here alone. My story ended the way it did because of some amazing and gifted people whom I can't thank enough for their support and just being a part of my life. You all mean the world to me.

My fabulous kids, Cambria, Christian, Evan, and Grace

My mom, Susan Coles

My hilarious dad, John Brooks, and his beautiful wife, Lisa

My excellent attorney, Glenn Massina

My wonderful friend, Jane Galli

My best bud, Jason Ward

My engineer, Vishaal Verma

My phenomenal friend, Kimberly Anderson, her husband, Blake, and their darling baby girl, Olivia

My amazing friends, Marc and Christina Hayford and their beautiful daughter, Jayda

My friends, Laurie and Tony and their wonderful children, Briton, Alana, and Lexi

My Kickstarter contributors

Rick Kelly

Lewis Gotch

Shelley Henshaw

ABC and *Funderdome* and the dynamic Steve Harvey

Dave Yonce

Gordon Law

Swimming Duck

Genimex, especially including Janice Zhao

Patrice Kelly

Manda Koss

Tri State Athletics

All the amazing women in Women in Toys, especially including Mary Kay Russell, Deb de Sherbinin, and Nancy Zwiers

Caitlin Gutekunst

Genna Rosenberg

The extra-special crew at Wicked Cool Toys, especially including Crystal Pizzullo, Stefanie Barone, Herb Mitschele, Bob Turner, David Schwartz, Kelly Foley, Colleen Veilleux, and Brittany Altmann

My amazing and fantastic partners, Michael Rinzler and Jeremy Padawer

The beautiful Princess T

My wonderful mentor and publisher, Arthur Klebanoff

My fabulous editor, Francine LaSala

The staff of RosettaBooks, especially including Brian Skulnik

My amazing publicist, Meryl Moss, and her wonderful team, Carole Claps and Sharon Geltner

Trinity Community Church

Jazwares

God, Jesus, and the Holy Spirit

Love you all! Thank you!

Angie

About the Author

Angie Cella is the president and chief dreamer at GEMC^2, and ERVP at Arbonne International. She is an inventor, entrepreneur, a woman of profound faith, and the mother of four awesome children. Throughout her career, she has dedicated herself to hard work and persistence, and to motivating and supporting others to achieve their own dreams.